Love Embers

Love Embers

A COLLECTION OF POETRY

BY

Mckennah Noh

ACKNOWLEDGEMENTS

MOM AND DAD

Thank you for bringing me into the world to be the strong minded and ambitious young women that I am today. Thank you for always instilling me with courage and most importantly faith and love. I couldn't be more thankful for the unique loving parents I have the honor to call mine.

ANGELA SOLIS

What can I say you were divine timing as we like to say to each other, but you truly were. I lost what true friendship meant but then I met you. Thank you for inspiring me to write this book. You sparked the idea and thus challenged me to truly go forward through another avenue to express myself and tell a story through art and feeling. Thank you for showing me that people can still pay attention to the little things in someone. Can still go out of one's way to make someone else's day. Thank you for showing me nothing but consistent, healthy, and real love in our friendship.
I thank God every day that he gave me you to share adventures, hardships, and beautiful memories within this life. Thank you for guiding me through this and being my best friend, my unexpected family, and my twin flame, not to mention my favorite Aries of all time.
—*I love ya Ang.*

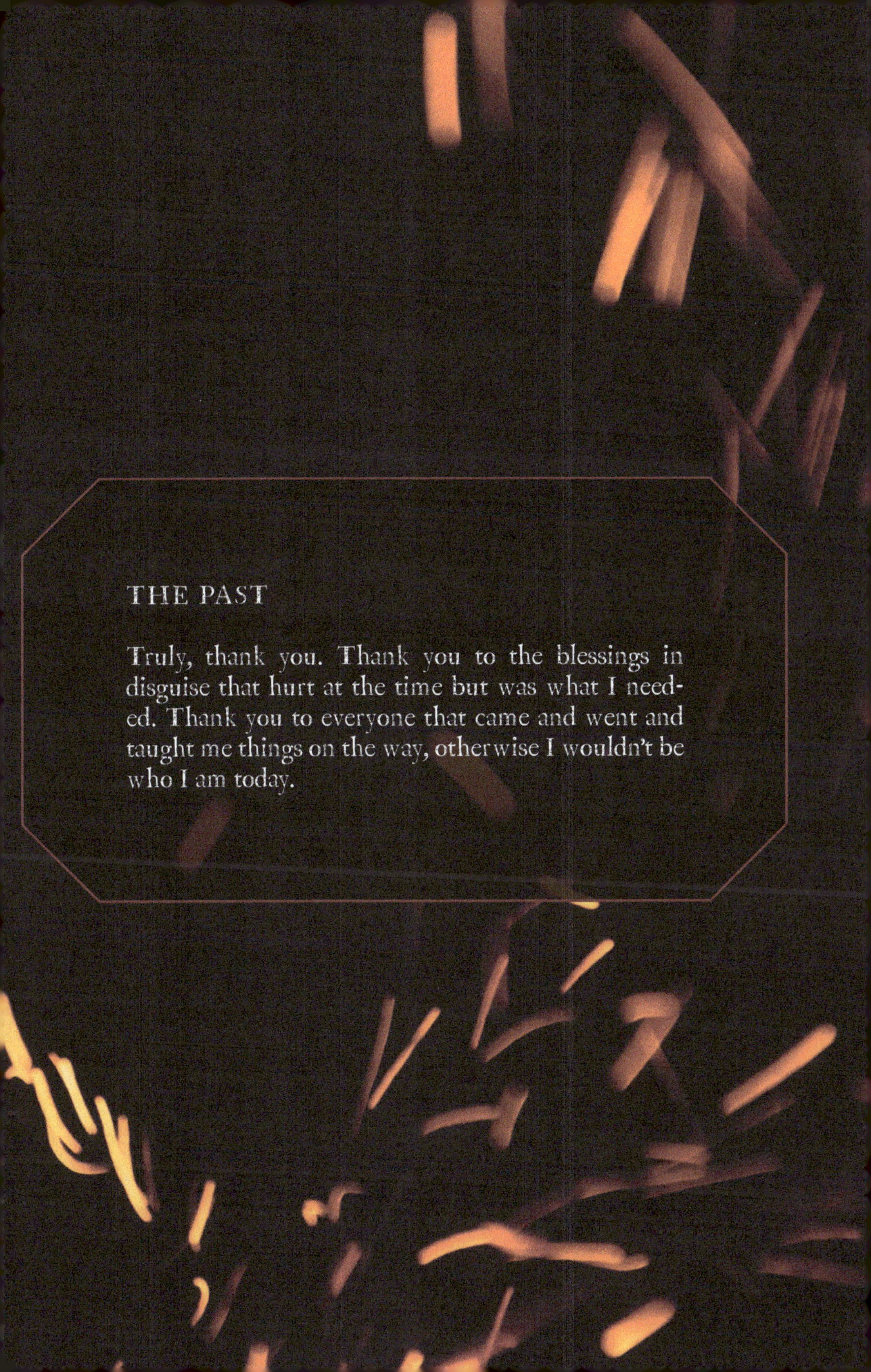

THE PAST

Truly, thank you. Thank you to the blessings in disguise that hurt at the time but was what I needed. Thank you to everyone that came and went and taught me things on the way, otherwise I wouldn't be who I am today.

FOREWORD

by Angela Solis

It's a beautiful sunny, 46-degree type of Sunday afternoon in March as I'm writing this on my couch while McKennah is asleep. So, here I am, finally writing as I've been thinking constantly about how I should approach this type of writing honor or let alone figure out where to start and how to give the proper appreciation that is her, without writing a whole novel and to just keep it short and sweet, but I think that's what makes this challenge even more beautiful to do.

You know, as a poet, I'm actually not very in tune with a lot of modern poets or connect with them on a level that I can understand, and if I do, I can count these Artists on only one hand, but with McKennah, ever since she started writing again, and as I have had the privilege to hear her mind in another art form, I connected instantaneously.

She has yet to cease to amaze me on how much her thoughts expand and how she is always so hungry to learn more about connection, the type that's beyond surface level, or wanting to untangle the mysterious untold wonders of this world, and wanting to constantly dissect more about herself. That type of growth, that type of self-love realization is the most precious and beautiful thing into this world. To be able to witness a young woman bloom and blossom into who she is meant to be is a treasure in my eyes. She has been like this ever since I had the blessing of meeting her in January of 2020 and that type of love for the world, for people, for herself has not stopped, I admire that beyond words.

But her words, I hope whoever is reading this will allow themselves to connect and become engulfed within this young woman's thoughts, messages and memories that she has written as much as I have because they are nothing short of honest. Poems that touch on the pain of letting go when that was never part of the plan, to the acceptance of knowing that there is light at the end of healing, to giving grace and forgiveness towards yourself for ever taking any treatment that was less than what you deserved, and to giving love that has finally focused inward unapologetically.

So, as you dive into this tangible piece of McKennah's mind, I hope that you find a safe space within her pages and feel comfort knowing that you are not alone.

- Angela Solis, author of *What Lies in the Wolf's Heart*, & *MANIC*.

Virginia, March, 2021

Dear Reader,

Ink dries, but the words within these lines will never die.
As you dive into this illuminated book of embers,
you will see many different perceptions of love.
It's not about the fuzzy middle school feelings
of what we all thought love meant,
it's about the gritty, uncomfortable, confusing,
painful yet beautiful and
inspiring truths that embody
the sacred four letter word

l
o
v
e

This book is a real and raw journey of the unpredictable stages of emotion and feeling that we humans take on when finding, feeling, or losing love, all through my personal story.

Enjoy.
Thank you for taking the journey with me.

— *McKennah Noh*

Love Embers

CONTENTS

Breathless
Smoke

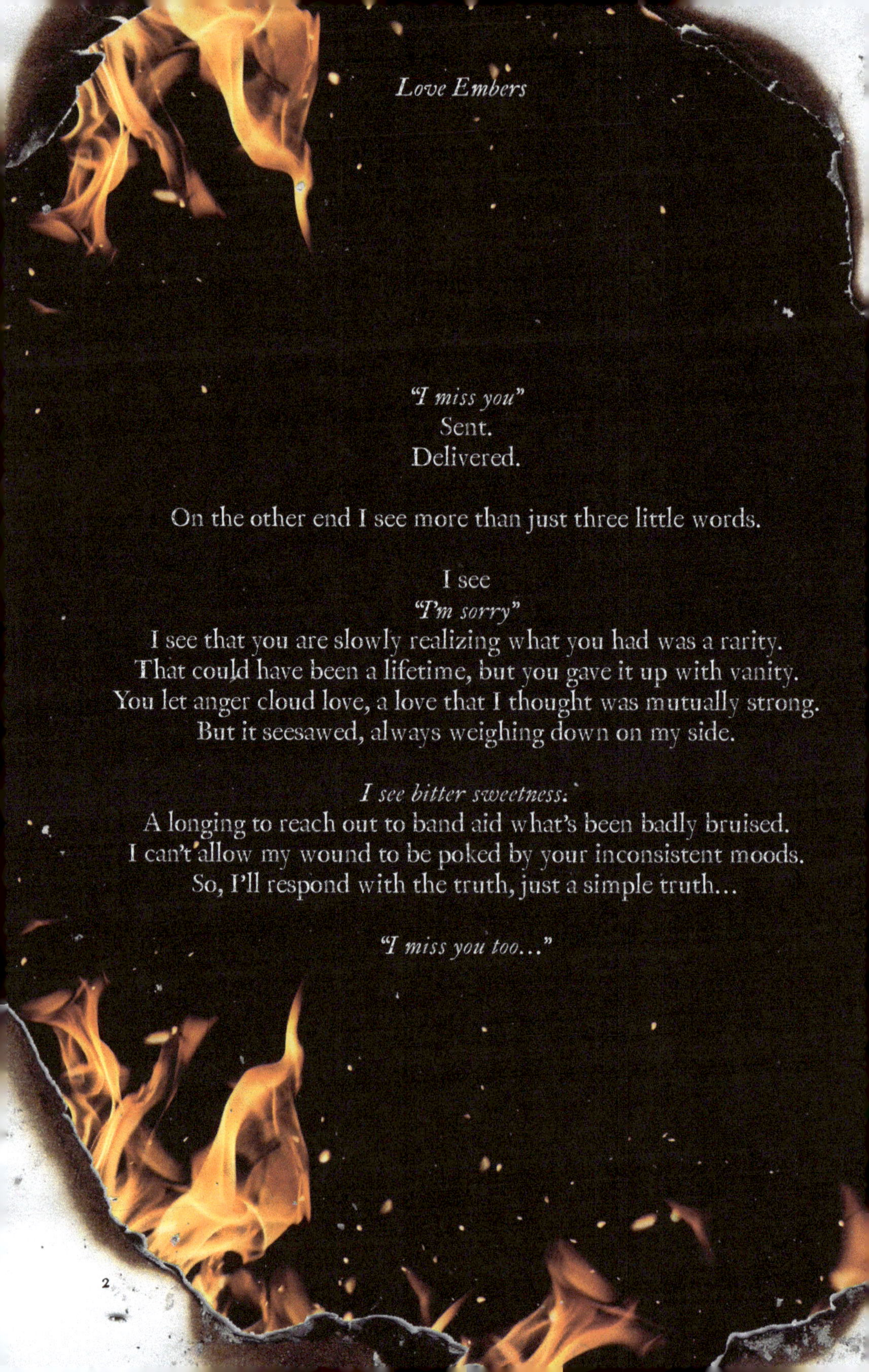

Love Embers

"I miss you"
Sent.
Delivered.

On the other end I see more than just three little words.

I see
"I'm sorry"
I see that you are slowly realizing what you had was a rarity.
That could have been a lifetime, but you gave it up with vanity.
You let anger cloud love, a love that I thought was mutually strong.
But it seesawed, always weighing down on my side.

I see bitter sweetness:
A longing to reach out to band aid what's been badly bruised.
I can't allow my wound to be poked by your inconsistent moods.
So, I'll respond with the truth, just a simple truth...

"I miss you too..."

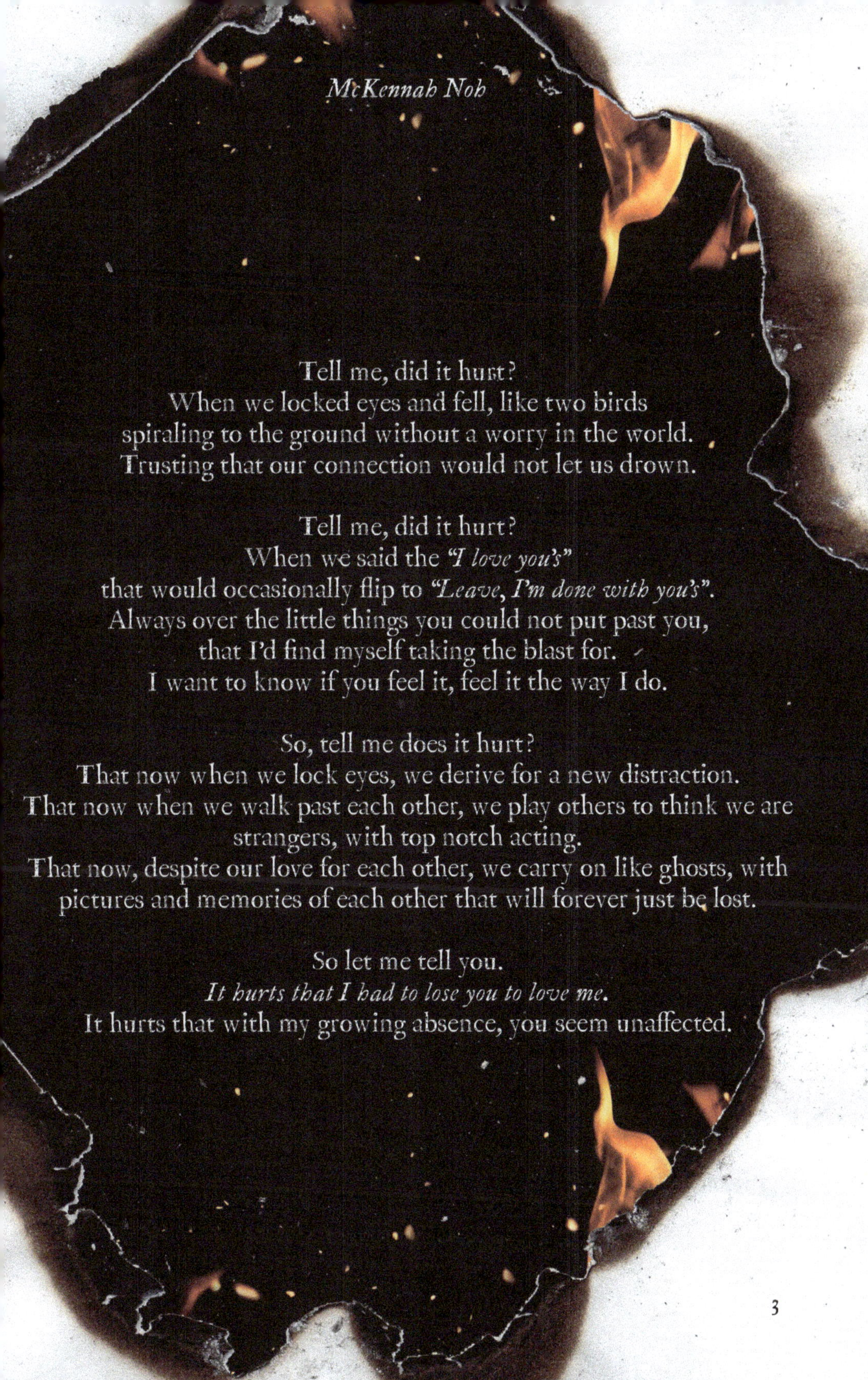

Tell me, did it hurt?
When we locked eyes and fell, like two birds
spiraling to the ground without a worry in the world.
Trusting that our connection would not let us drown.

Tell me, did it hurt?
When we said the *"I love you's"*
that would occasionally flip to *"Leave, I'm done with you's"*.
Always over the little things you could not put past you,
that I'd find myself taking the blast for.
I want to know if you feel it, feel it the way I do.

So, tell me does it hurt?
That now when we lock eyes, we derive for a new distraction.
That now when we walk past each other, we play others to think we are
strangers, with top notch acting.
That now, despite our love for each other, we carry on like ghosts, with
pictures and memories of each other that will forever just be lost.

So let me tell you.
It hurts that I had to lose you to love me.
It hurts that with my growing absence, you seem unaffected.

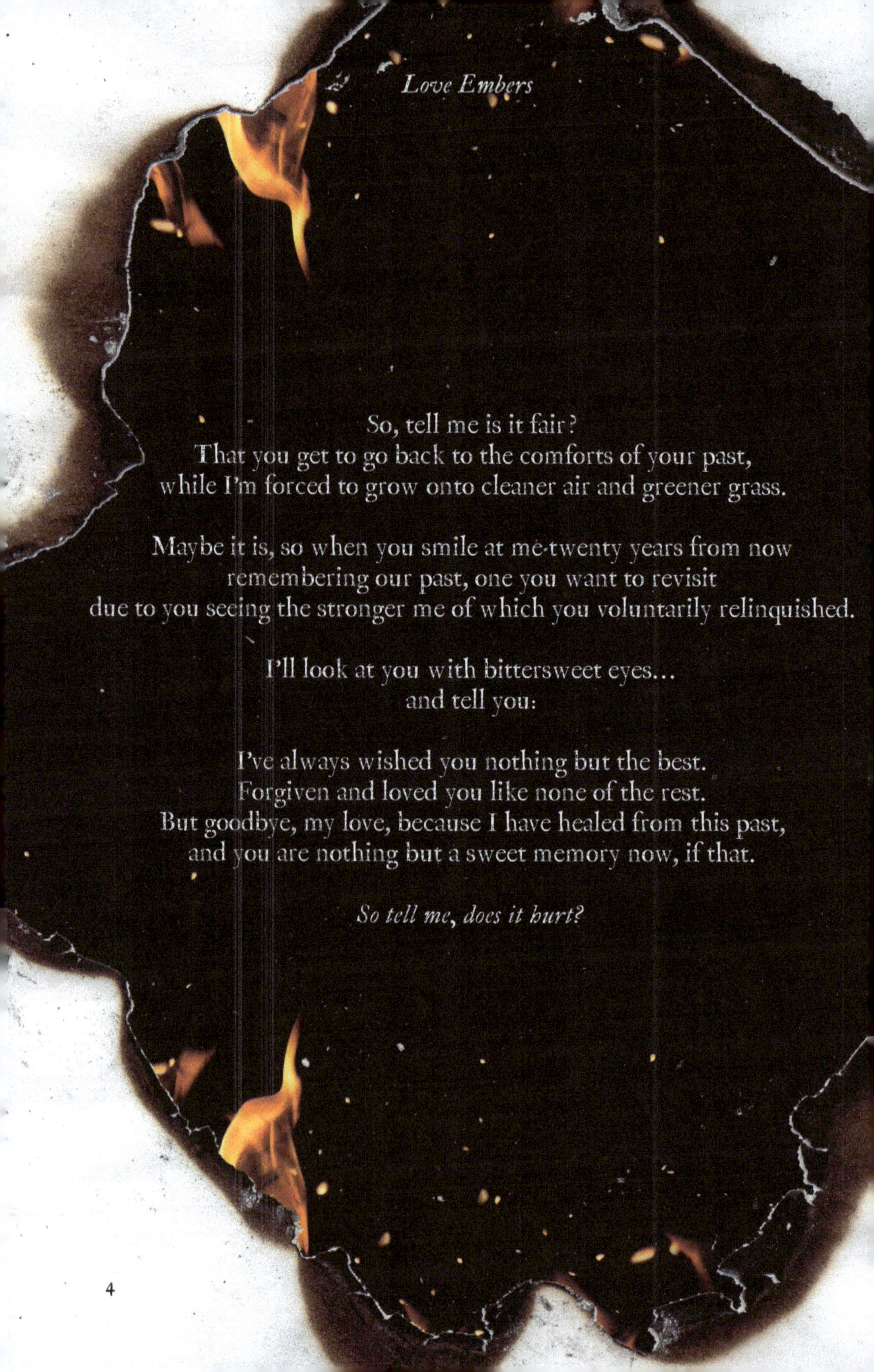

So, tell me is it fair?
That you get to go back to the comforts of your past,
while I'm forced to grow onto cleaner air and greener grass.

Maybe it is, so when you smile at me twenty years from now
remembering our past, one you want to revisit
due to you seeing the stronger me of which you voluntarily relinquished.

I'll look at you with bittersweet eyes…
and tell you:

I've always wished you nothing but the best.
Forgiven and loved you like none of the rest.
But goodbye, my love, because I have healed from this past,
and you are nothing but a sweet memory now, if that.

So tell me, does it hurt?

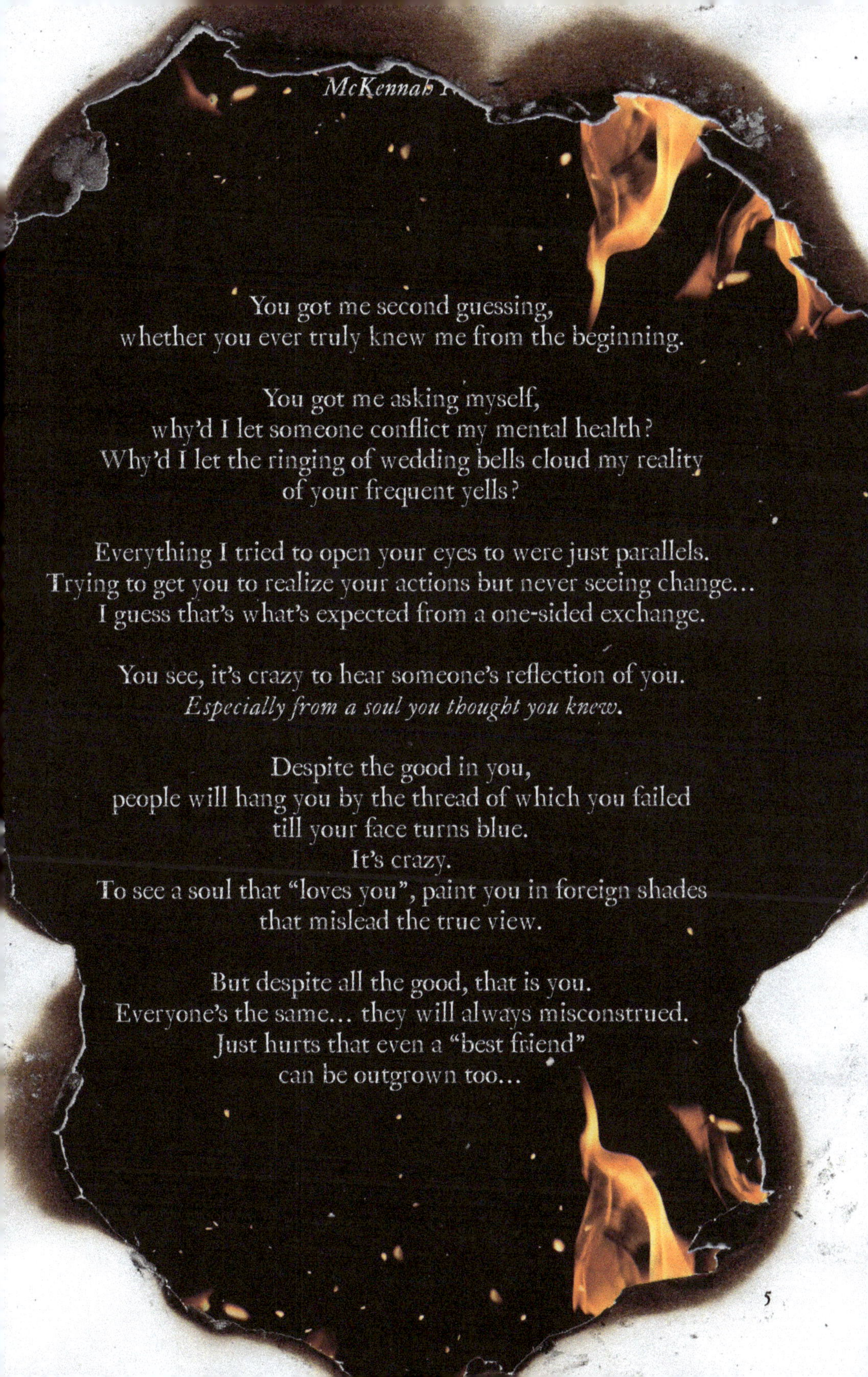

You got me second guessing,
whether you ever truly knew me from the beginning.

You got me asking myself,
why'd I let someone conflict my mental health?
Why'd I let the ringing of wedding bells cloud my reality
of your frequent yells?

Everything I tried to open your eyes to were just parallels.
Trying to get you to realize your actions but never seeing change…
I guess that's what's expected from a one-sided exchange.

You see, it's crazy to hear someone's reflection of you.
Especially from a soul you thought you knew.

Despite the good in you,
people will hang you by the thread of which you failed
till your face turns blue.
It's crazy.
To see a soul that "loves you", paint you in foreign shades
that mislead the true view.

But despite all the good, that is you.
Everyone's the same… they will always misconstrued.
Just hurts that even a "best friend"
can be outgrown too…

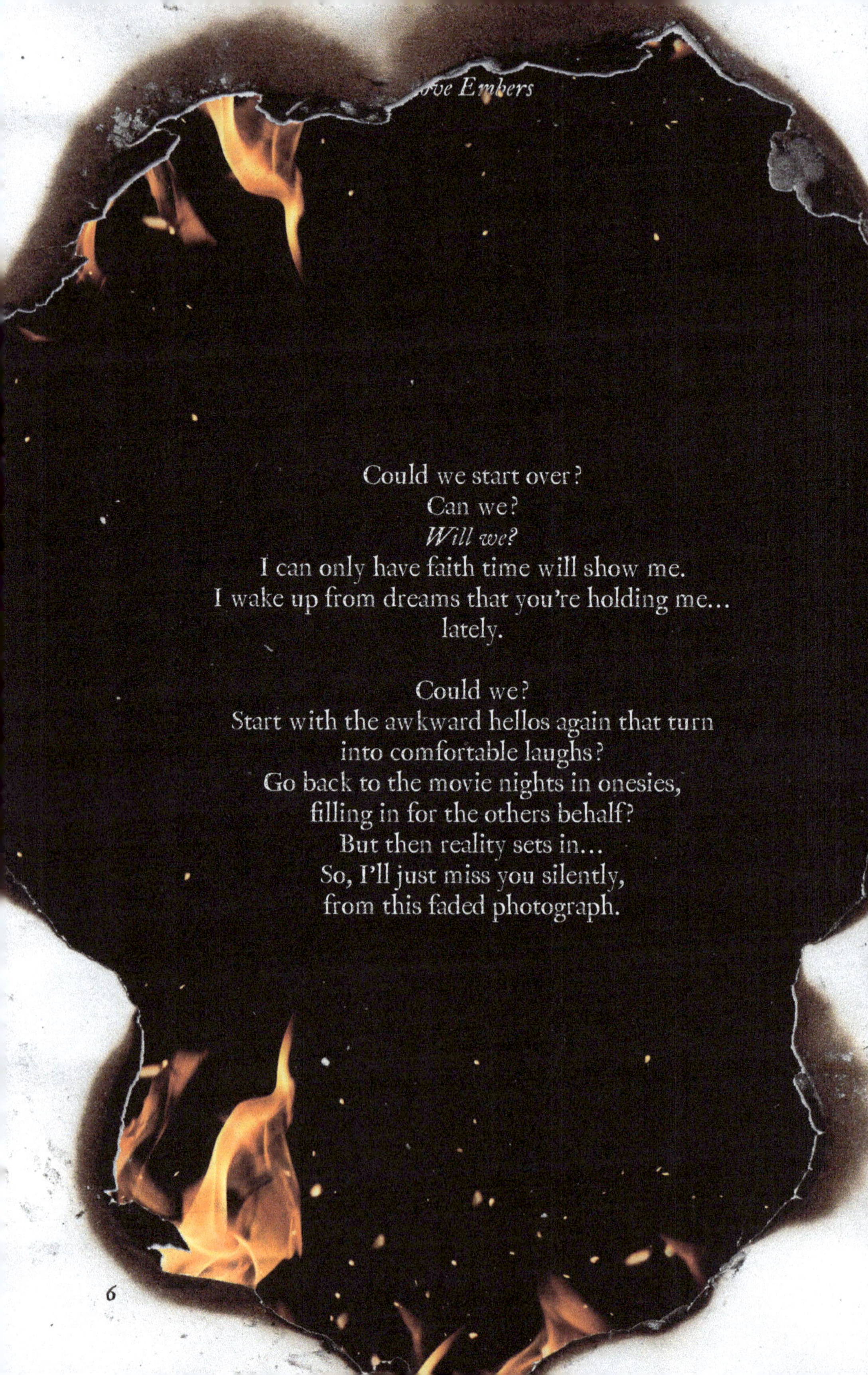

Could we start over?
Can we?
Will we?
I can only have faith time will show me.
I wake up from dreams that you're holding me…
lately.

Could we?
Start with the awkward hellos again that turn
into comfortable laughs?
Go back to the movie nights in onesies,
filling in for the others behalf?
But then reality sets in…
So, I'll just miss you silently,
from this faded photograph.

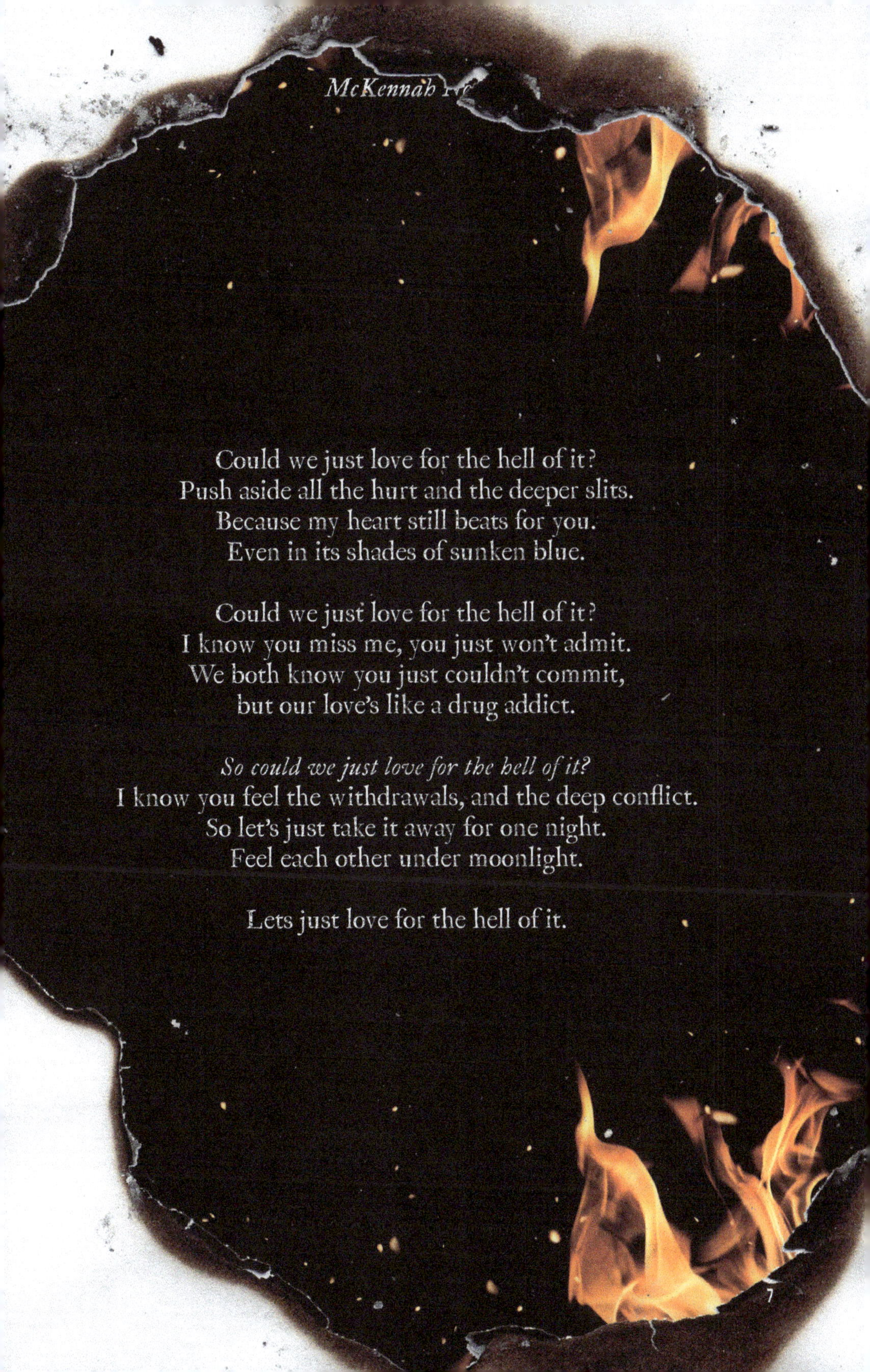

Could we just love for the hell of it?
Push aside all the hurt and the deeper slits.
Because my heart still beats for you.
Even in its shades of sunken blue.

Could we just love for the hell of it?
I know you miss me, you just won't admit.
We both know you just couldn't commit,
but our love's like a drug addict.

So could we just love for the hell of it?
I know you feel the withdrawals, and the deep conflict.
So let's just take it away for one night.
Feel each other under moonlight.

Lets just love for the hell of it.

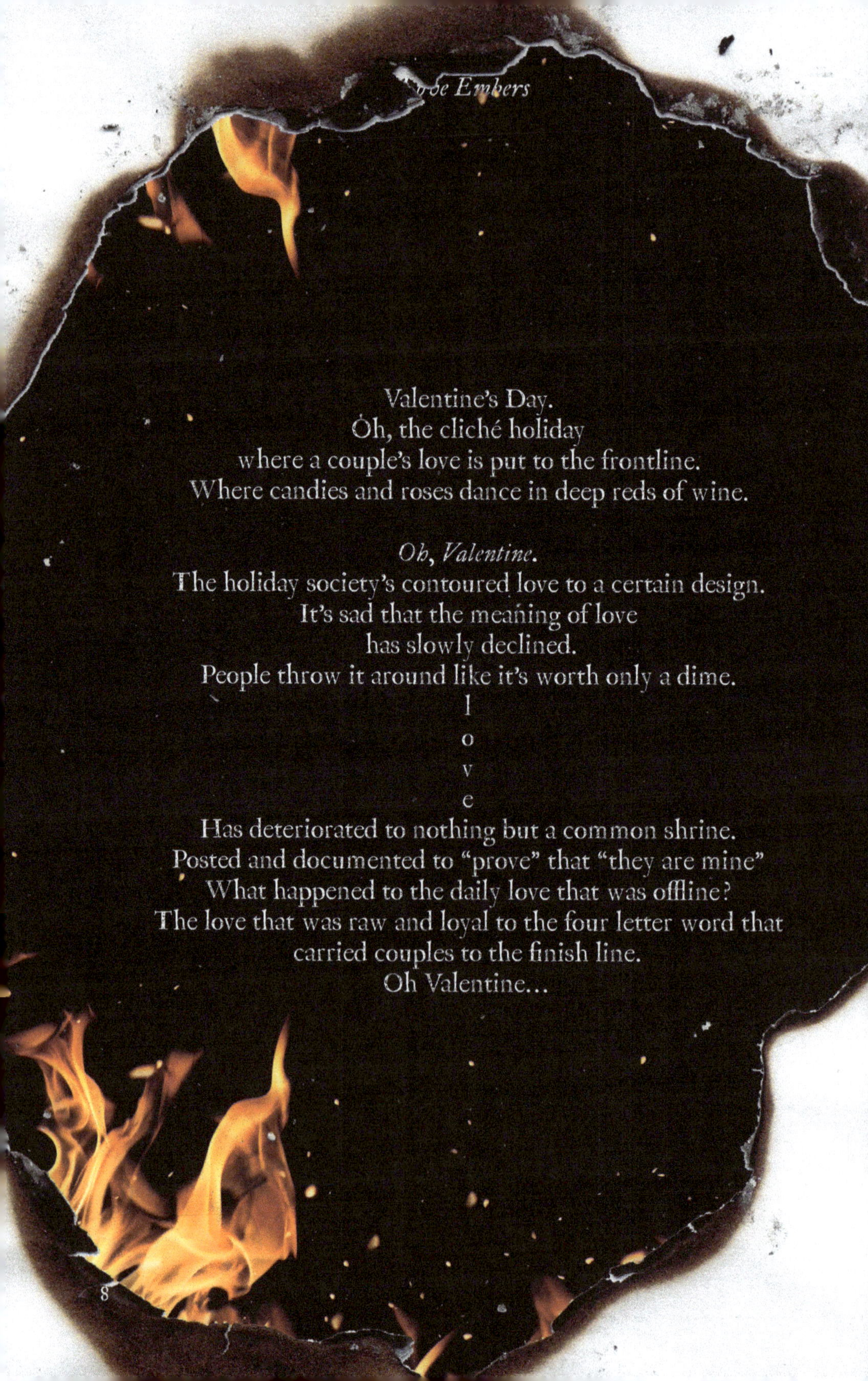

Valentine's Day.
Oh, the cliché holiday
where a couple's love is put to the frontline.
Where candies and roses dance in deep reds of wine.

Oh, Valentine.
The holiday society's contoured love to a certain design.
It's sad that the meaning of love
has slowly declined.
People throw it around like it's worth only a dime.
l
o
v
e

Has deteriorated to nothing but a common shrine.
Posted and documented to "prove" that "they are mine"
What happened to the daily love that was offline?
The love that was raw and loyal to the four letter word that
carried couples to the finish line.
Oh Valentine...

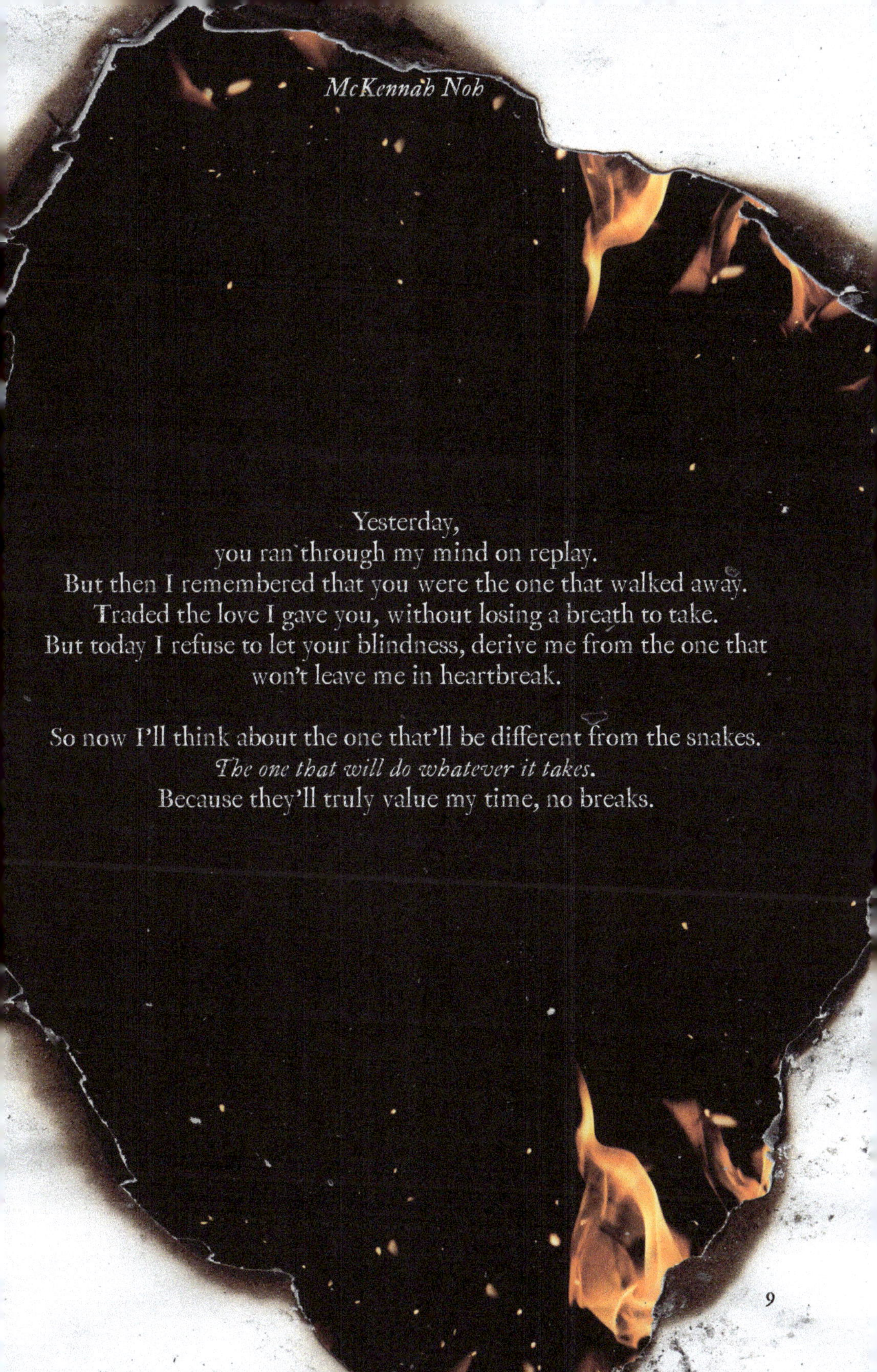

Yesterday,
you ran through my mind on replay.
But then I remembered that you were the one that walked away.
Traded the love I gave you, without losing a breath to take.
But today I refuse to let your blindness, derive me from the one that
won't leave me in heartbreak.

So now I'll think about the one that'll be different from the snakes.
The one that will do whatever it takes.
Because they'll truly value my time, no breaks.

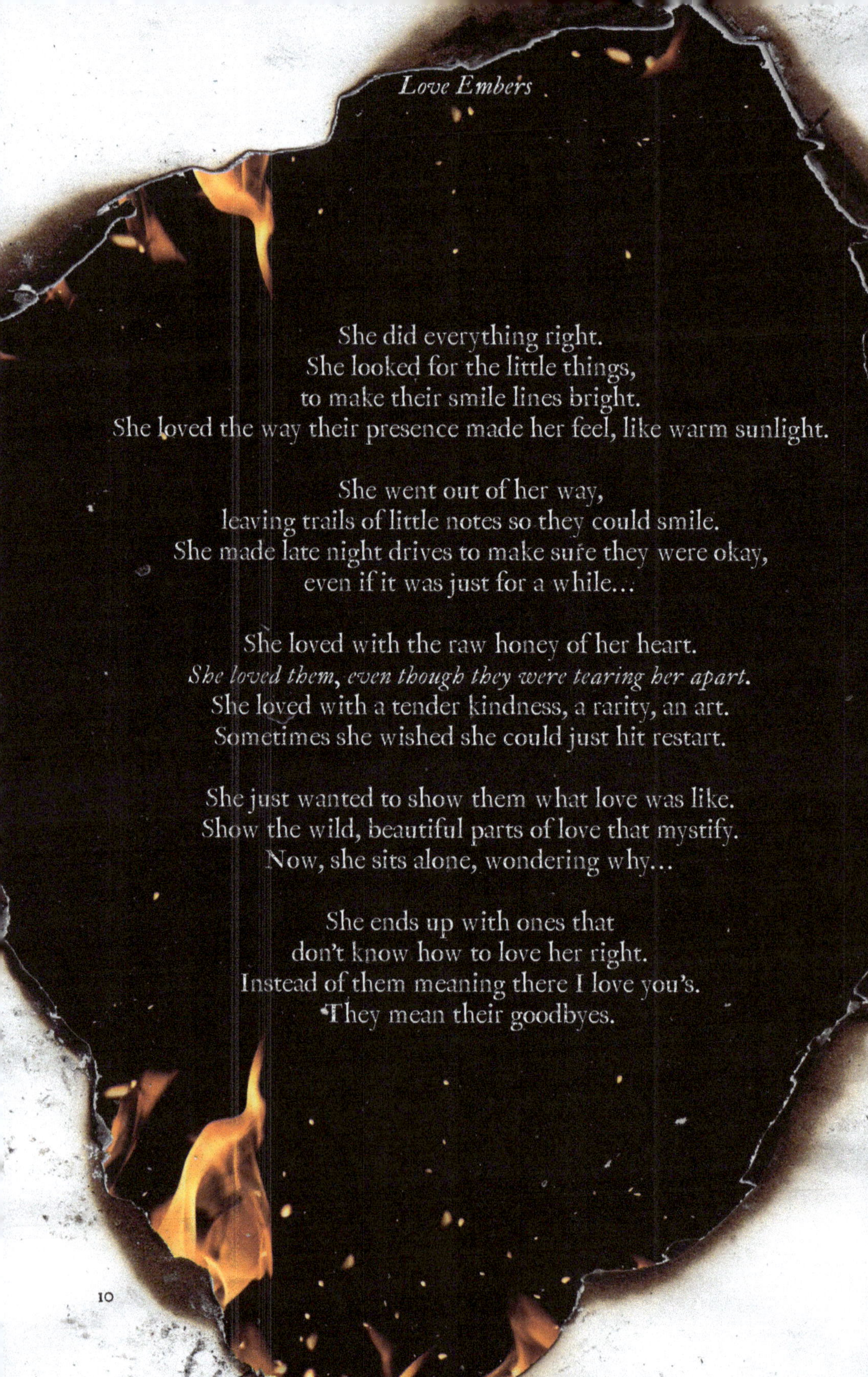

She did everything right.
She looked for the little things,
to make their smile lines bright.
She loved the way their presence made her feel, like warm sunlight.

She went out of her way,
leaving trails of little notes so they could smile.
She made late night drives to make sure they were okay,
even if it was just for a while…

She loved with the raw honey of her heart.
She loved them, even though they were tearing her apart.
She loved with a tender kindness, a rarity, an art.
Sometimes she wished she could just hit restart.

She just wanted to show them what love was like.
Show the wild, beautiful parts of love that mystify.
Now, she sits alone, wondering why…

She ends up with ones that
don't know how to love her right.
Instead of them meaning there I love you's.
They mean their goodbyes.

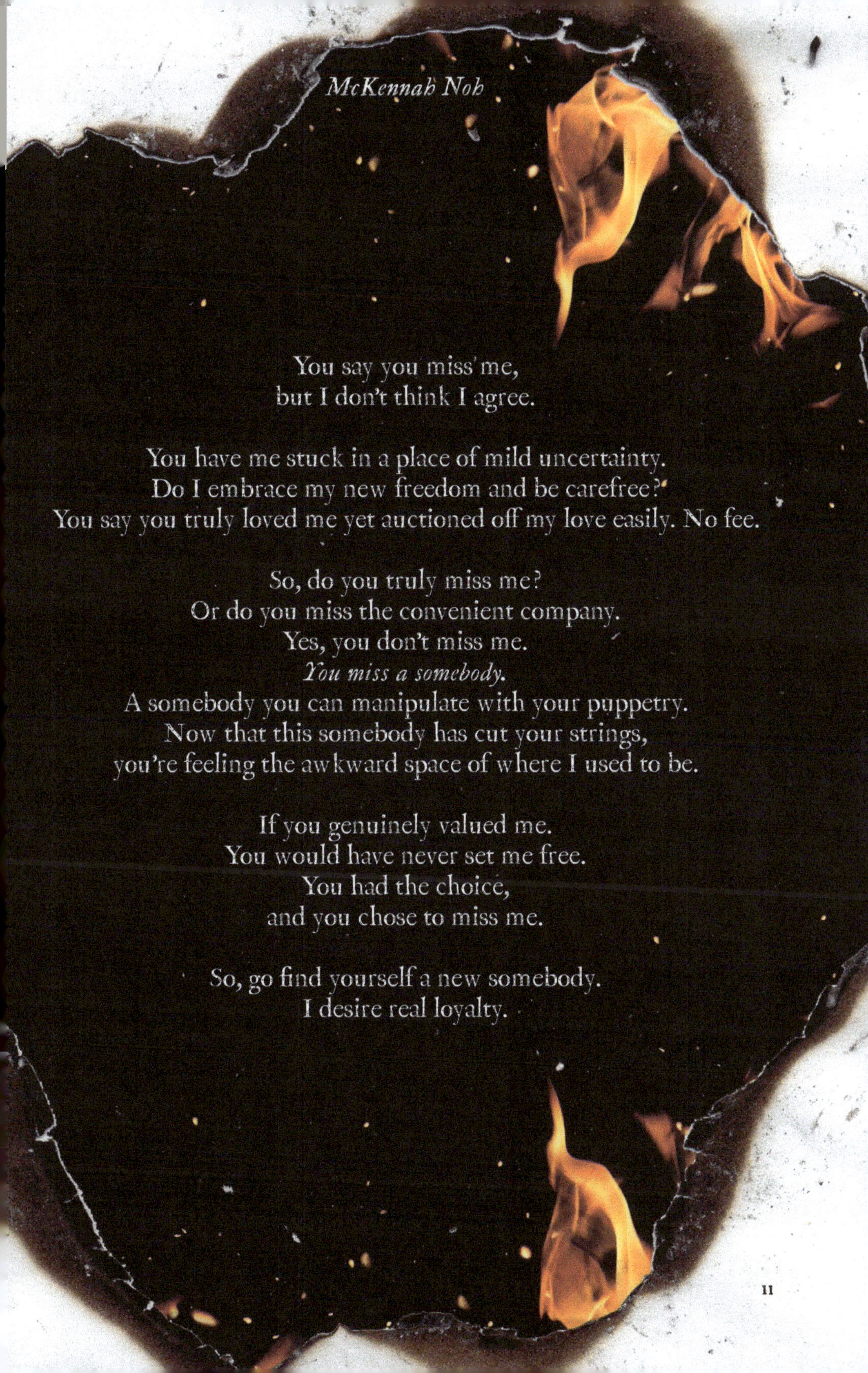

McKennah Noh

You say you miss me,
but I don't think I agree.

You have me stuck in a place of mild uncertainty.
Do I embrace my new freedom and be carefree?
You say you truly loved me yet auctioned off my love easily. No fee.

So, do you truly miss me?
Or do you miss the convenient company.
Yes, you don't miss me.
You miss a somebody.
A somebody you can manipulate with your puppetry.
Now that this somebody has cut your strings,
you're feeling the awkward space of where I used to be.

If you genuinely valued me.
You would have never set me free.
You had the choice,
and you chose to miss me.

So, go find yourself a new somebody.
I desire real loyalty.

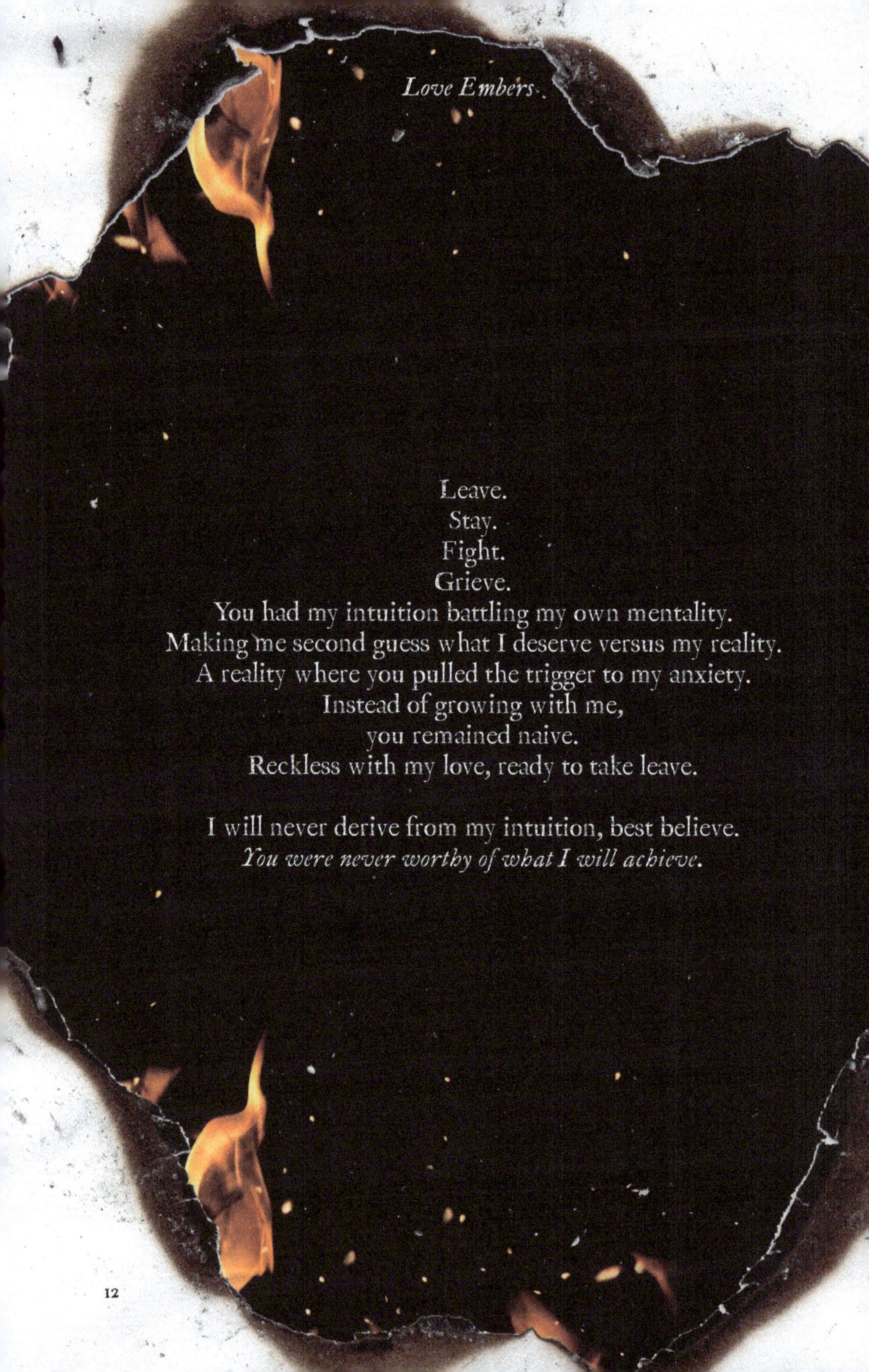
Love Embers.

Leave.
Stay.
Fight.
Grieve.
You had my intuition battling my own mentality.
Making me second guess what I deserve versus my reality.
A reality where you pulled the trigger to my anxiety.
Instead of growing with me,
you remained naive.
Reckless with my love, ready to take leave.

I will never derive from my intuition, best believe.
You were never worthy of what I will achieve.

McKennah Noh

It's crazy.
One day they're your everything.
The next they're a stranger.
A memory with all your secrets
that are now endangered.

13

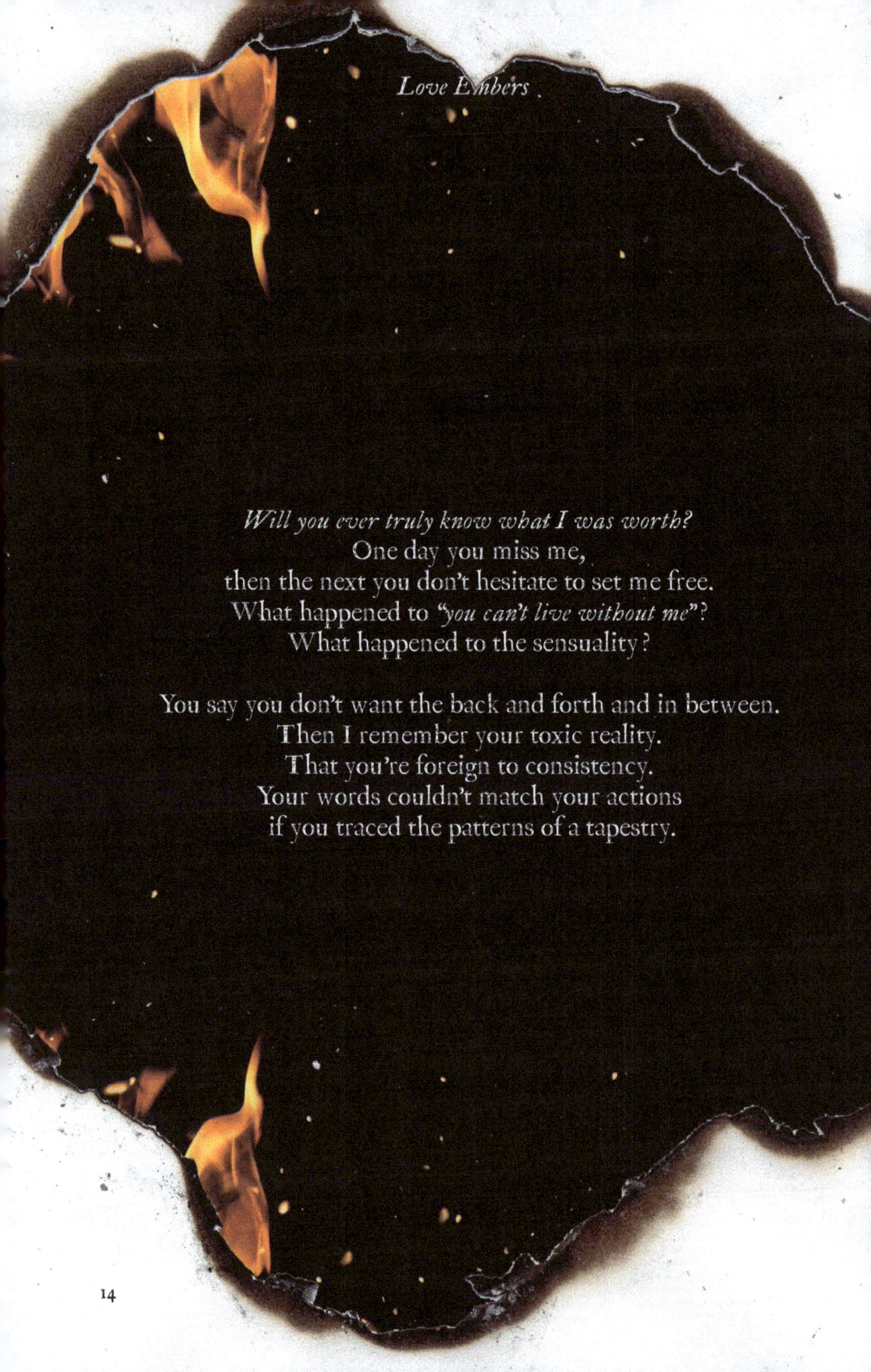

Love Embers

Will you ever truly know what I was worth?
One day you miss me,
then the next you don't hesitate to set me free.
What happened to "you can't live without me"?
What happened to the sensuality?

You say you don't want the back and forth and in between.
Then I remember your toxic reality.
That you're foreign to consistency.
Your words couldn't match your actions
if you traced the patterns of a tapestry.

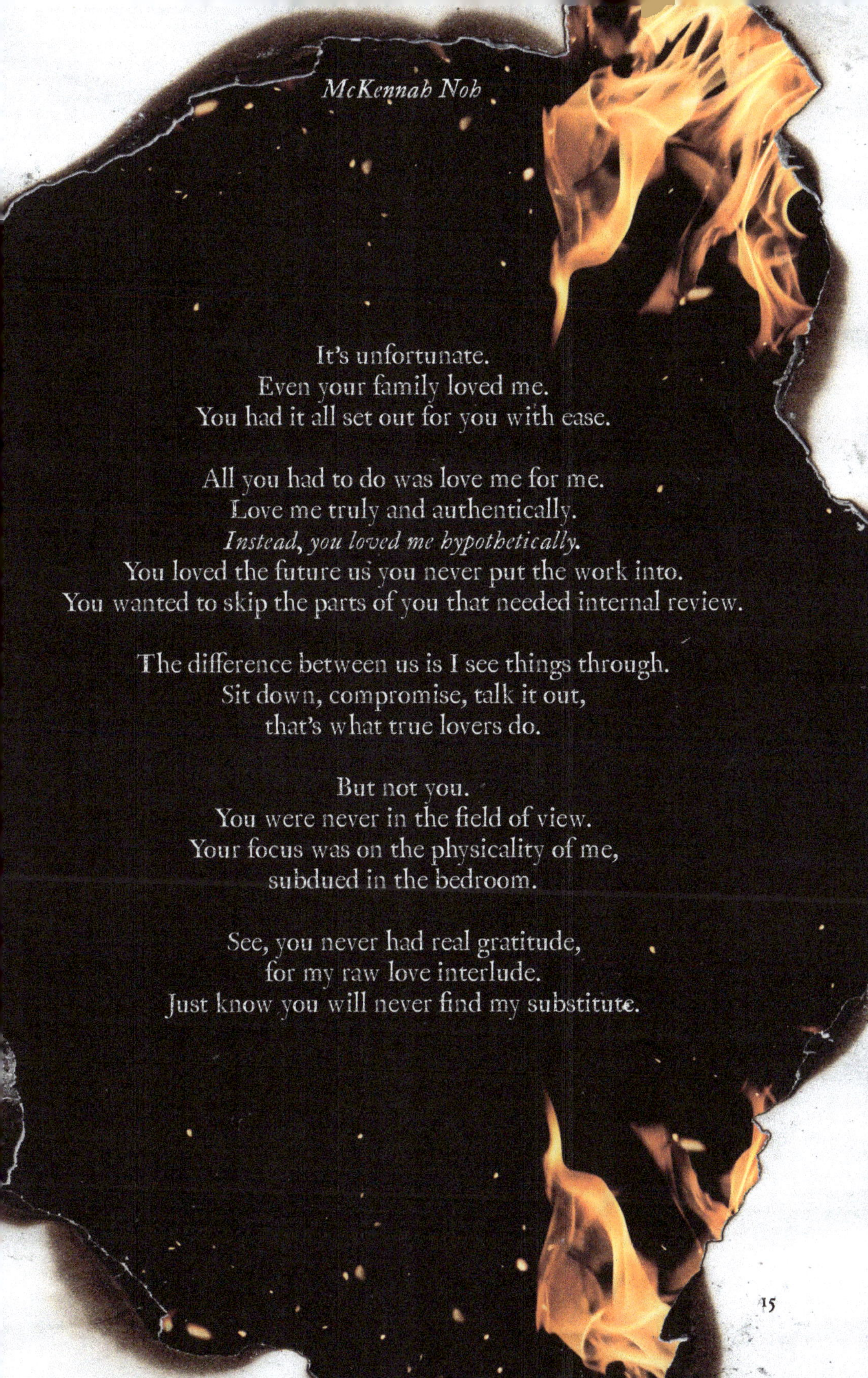

It's unfortunate.
Even your family loved me.
You had it all set out for you with ease.

All you had to do was love me for me.
Love me truly and authentically.
Instead, you loved me hypothetically.
You loved the future us you never put the work into.
You wanted to skip the parts of you that needed internal review.

The difference between us is I see things through.
Sit down, compromise, talk it out,
that's what true lovers do.

But not you.
You were never in the field of view.
Your focus was on the physicality of me,
subdued in the bedroom.

See, you never had real gratitude,
for my raw love interlude.
Just know you will never find my substitute.

But don't worry, babe,
don't get it confused.
I enjoy my newfound solitude.
At least now, I am immune.
Immune from the excuses you loved to cloak with your perfume,
hoping I'd come back to you.

But let me remind you,
you had your chances.
You could have had that future with me, but you never followed
through.
Your definition of loving someone is dressed in a costume.
Giving off false expectations, baby, you're see through.

God used me to teach you,
so don't worry, I've pushed through.
You were just a chapter that
hit me out of the blue.

But I'm thankful for your mistake,
because I know I grew.

So I'll continue to wish you the best,
even though your lack of effort and self-reflection had me oppressed.
Thank you for showing me I needed to reinvest.
In myself, and those who know when they are blessed.
But hey, don't stress.
Your mama still loves me, nonetheless.

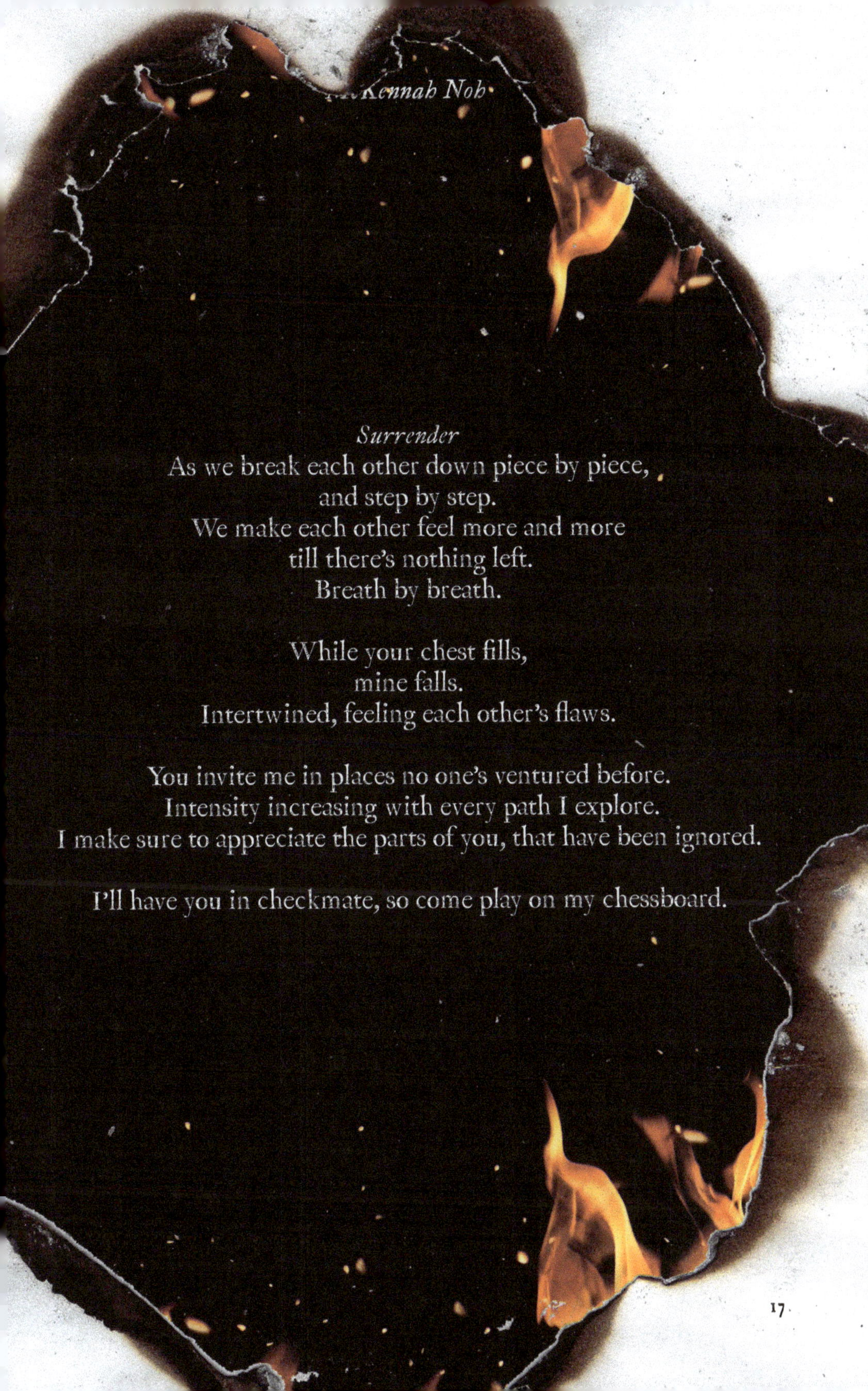

Surrender
As we break each other down piece by piece,
and step by step.
We make each other feel more and more
till there's nothing left.
Breath by breath.

While your chest fills,
mine falls.
Intertwined, feeling each other's flaws.

You invite me in places no one's ventured before.
Intensity increasing with every path I explore.
I make sure to appreciate the parts of you, that have been ignored.

I'll have you in checkmate, so come play on my chessboard.

I know you're no good for me,
yet I stay to see if you will turn out to be
the person
that will add a seed to my family tree.

But deep down I know this is just a love tale tragedy.

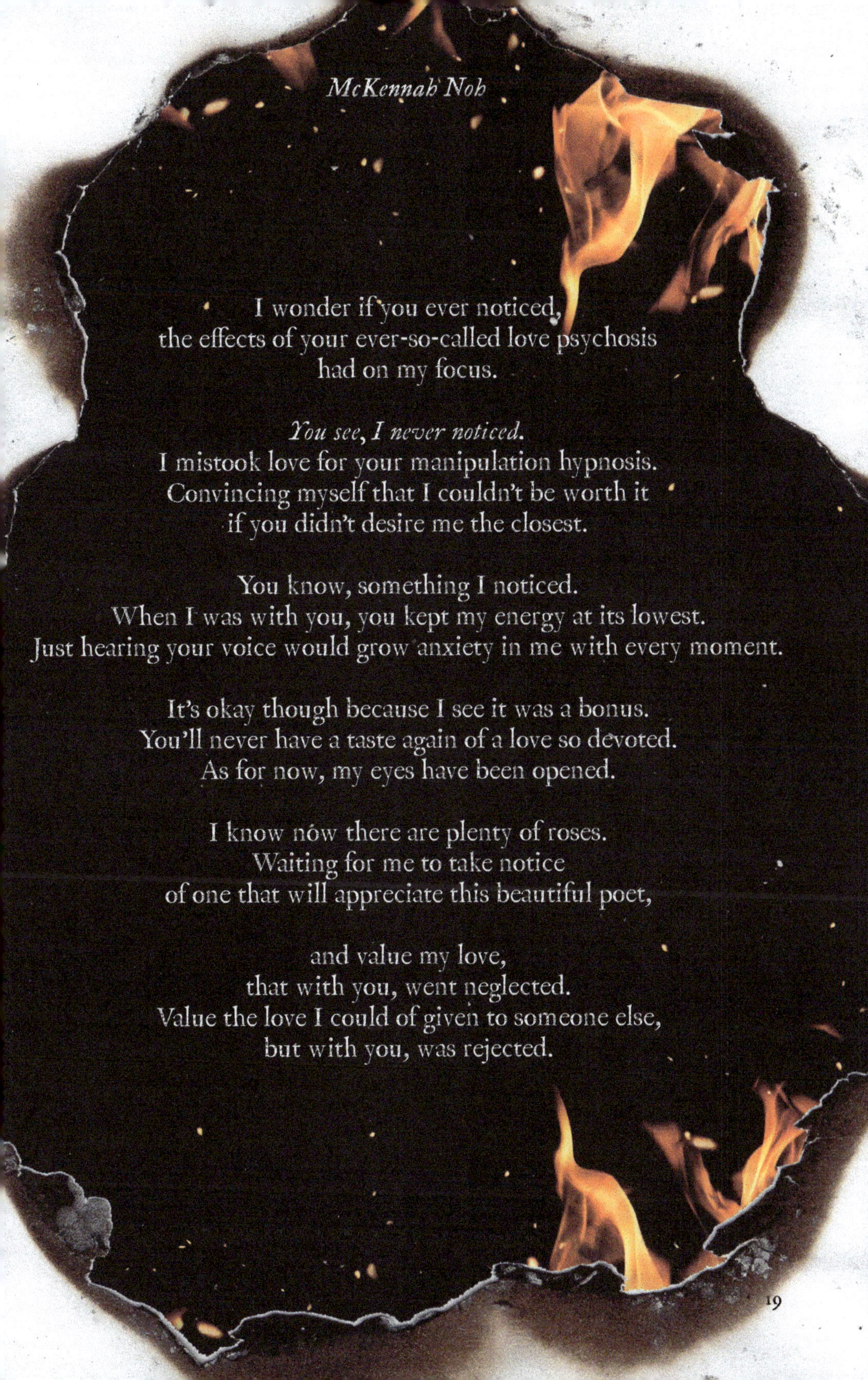

McKennah Noh

I wonder if you ever noticed,
the effects of your ever-so-called love psychosis
had on my focus.

You see, I never noticed.
I mistook love for your manipulation hypnosis.
Convincing myself that I couldn't be worth it
if you didn't desire me the closest.

You know, something I noticed.
When I was with you, you kept my energy at its lowest.
Just hearing your voice would grow anxiety in me with every moment.

It's okay though because I see it was a bonus.
You'll never have a taste again of a love so devoted.
As for now, my eyes have been opened.

I know now there are plenty of roses.
Waiting for me to take notice
of one that will appreciate this beautiful poet,

and value my love,
that with you, went neglected.
Value the love I could of given to someone else,
but with you, was rejected.

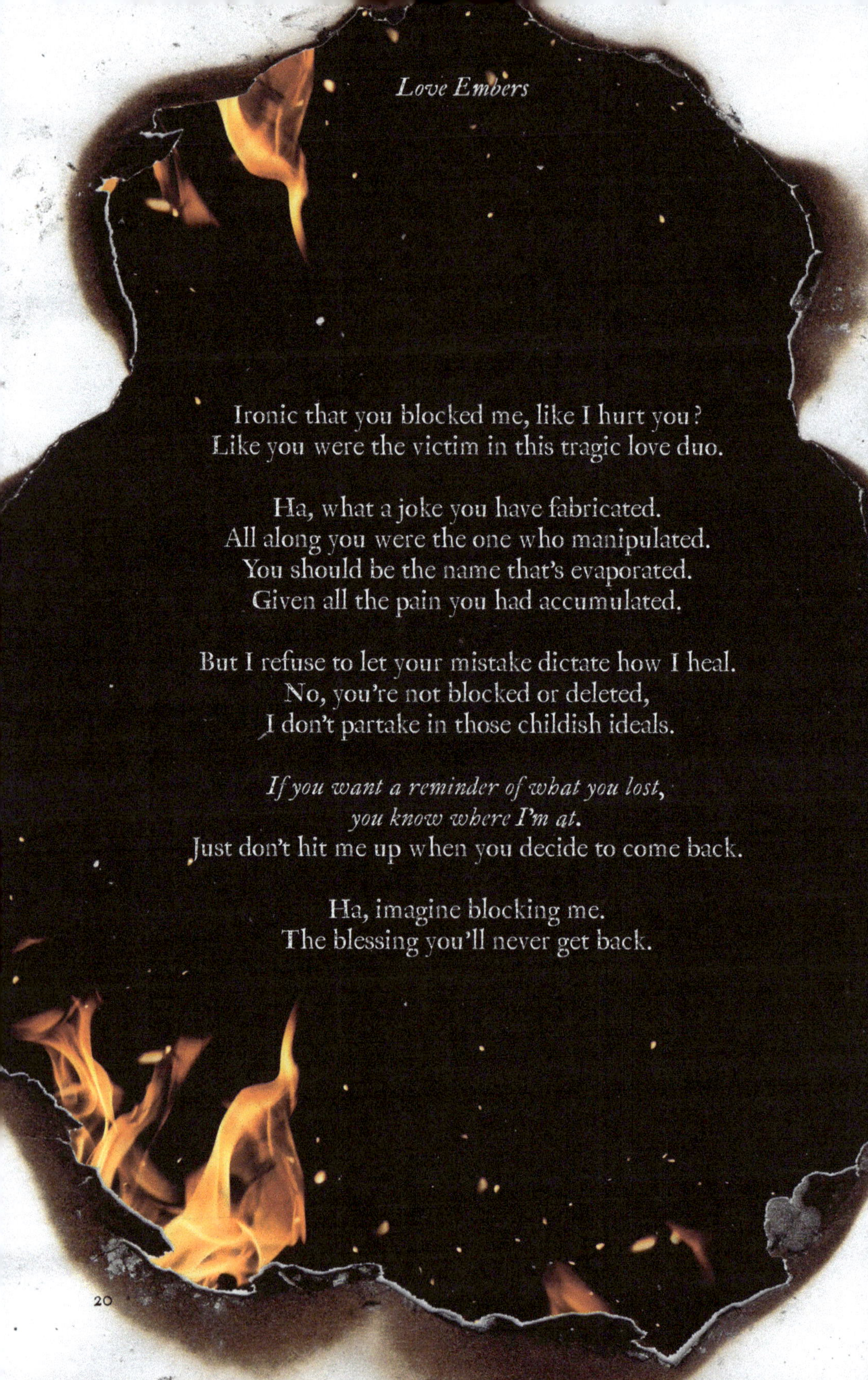

Love Embers

Ironic that you blocked me, like I hurt you?
Like you were the victim in this tragic love duo.

Ha, what a joke you have fabricated.
All along you were the one who manipulated.
You should be the name that's evaporated.
Given all the pain you had accumulated.

But I refuse to let your mistake dictate how I heal.
No, you're not blocked or deleted,
I don't partake in those childish ideals.

If you want a reminder of what you lost,
you know where I'm at.
Just don't hit me up when you decide to come back.

Ha, imagine blocking me.
The blessing you'll never get back.

20

McKennah Noh

A broken marriage...
Hardest thing to witness
when it used to be something that was cherished.
Two beautiful souls getting lost in the wreckage,
of insignificant arguments blowing up within seconds.

To see how numb they are to the impacts,
that their toxic traits and words of venom
have left their kids in aftermath.
How could you look at the person you married and tell them to die,
let alone wish that on any human beings' soul,
I just wish you could tell me why?

Why can't you just change for the better?
It's like you want to be bitter forever.
You don't even understand how much I wish to see you happy,
but it kills me inside every time you show me your truth
it's disgusting and trashy.

How did I end up with the heart that I have?
If I came from two people who can't even move on from the past.

Fuck! It's like all those nights I've wasted.
Ha, I really thought you appreciated my wisdoms basics,
but you continue to leave me devastated,
with the lack of growth and effort, you make it complicated.

It sucks because I know deep down you're just hurt and frustrated,
but I just can't give you any excuses anymore
for the way you've alienated.

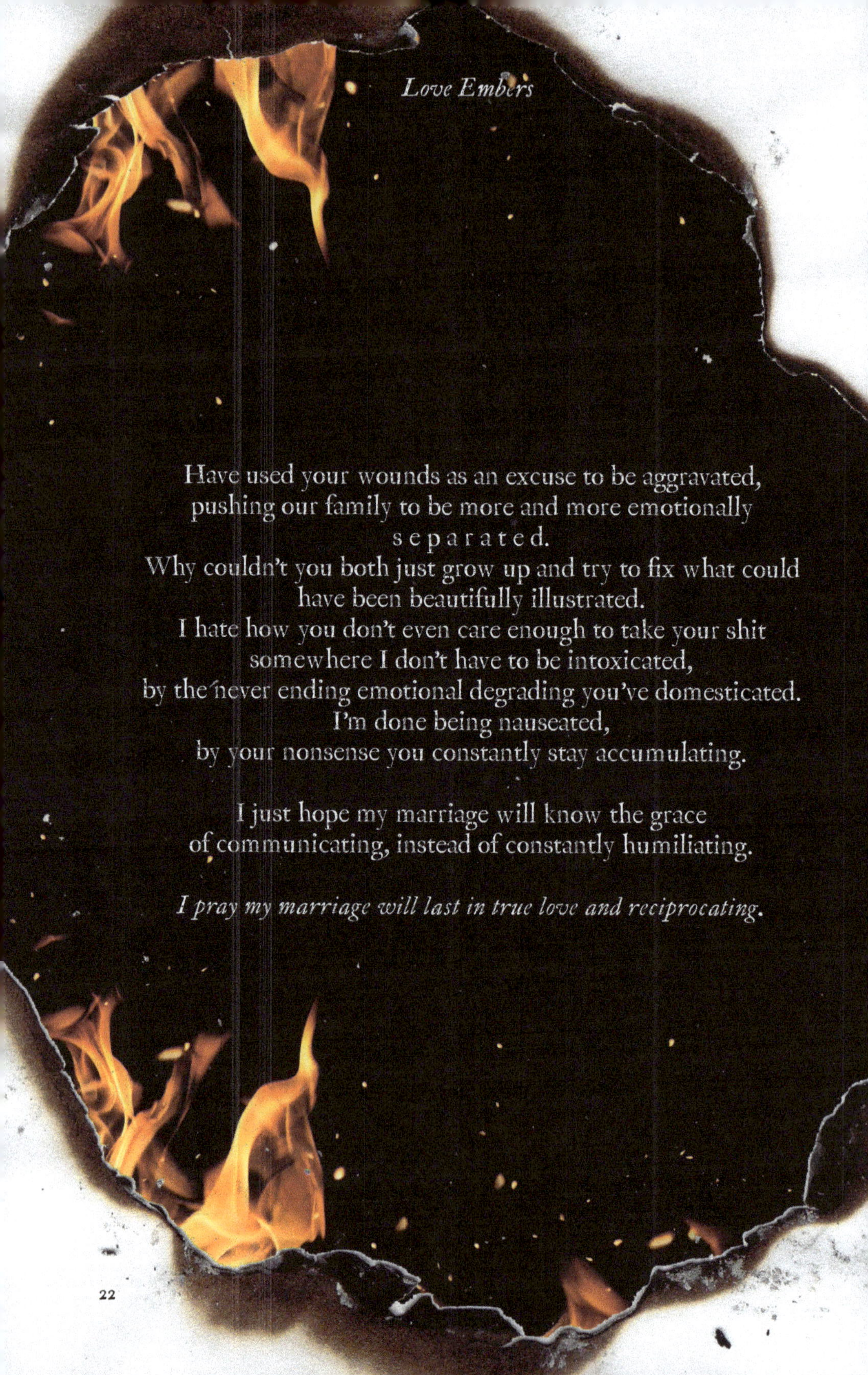

Have used your wounds as an excuse to be aggravated,
pushing our family to be more and more emotionally
s e p a r a t e d.
Why couldn't you both just grow up and try to fix what could
have been beautifully illustrated.
I hate how you don't even care enough to take your shit
somewhere I don't have to be intoxicated,
by the never ending emotional degrading you've domesticated.
I'm done being nauseated,
by your nonsense you constantly stay accumulating.

I just hope my marriage will know the grace
of communicating, instead of constantly humiliating.

I pray my marriage will last in true love and reciprocating.

Cautious
Cinders

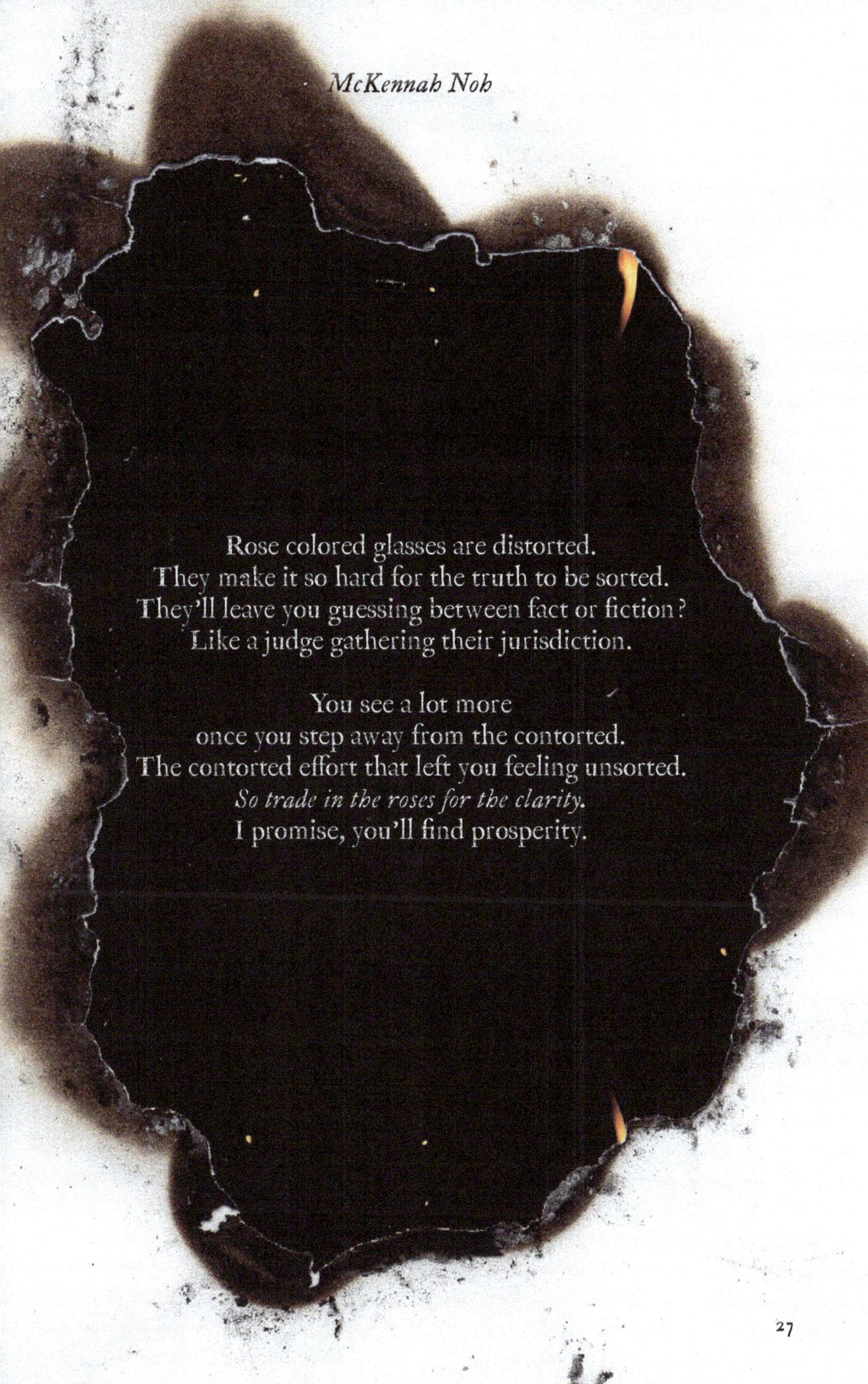

Rose colored glasses are distorted.
They make it so hard for the truth to be sorted.
They'll leave you guessing between fact or fiction?
Like a judge gathering their jurisdiction.

You see a lot more
once you step away from the contorted.
The contorted effort that left you feeling unsorted.
So trade in the roses for the clarity.
I promise, you'll find prosperity.

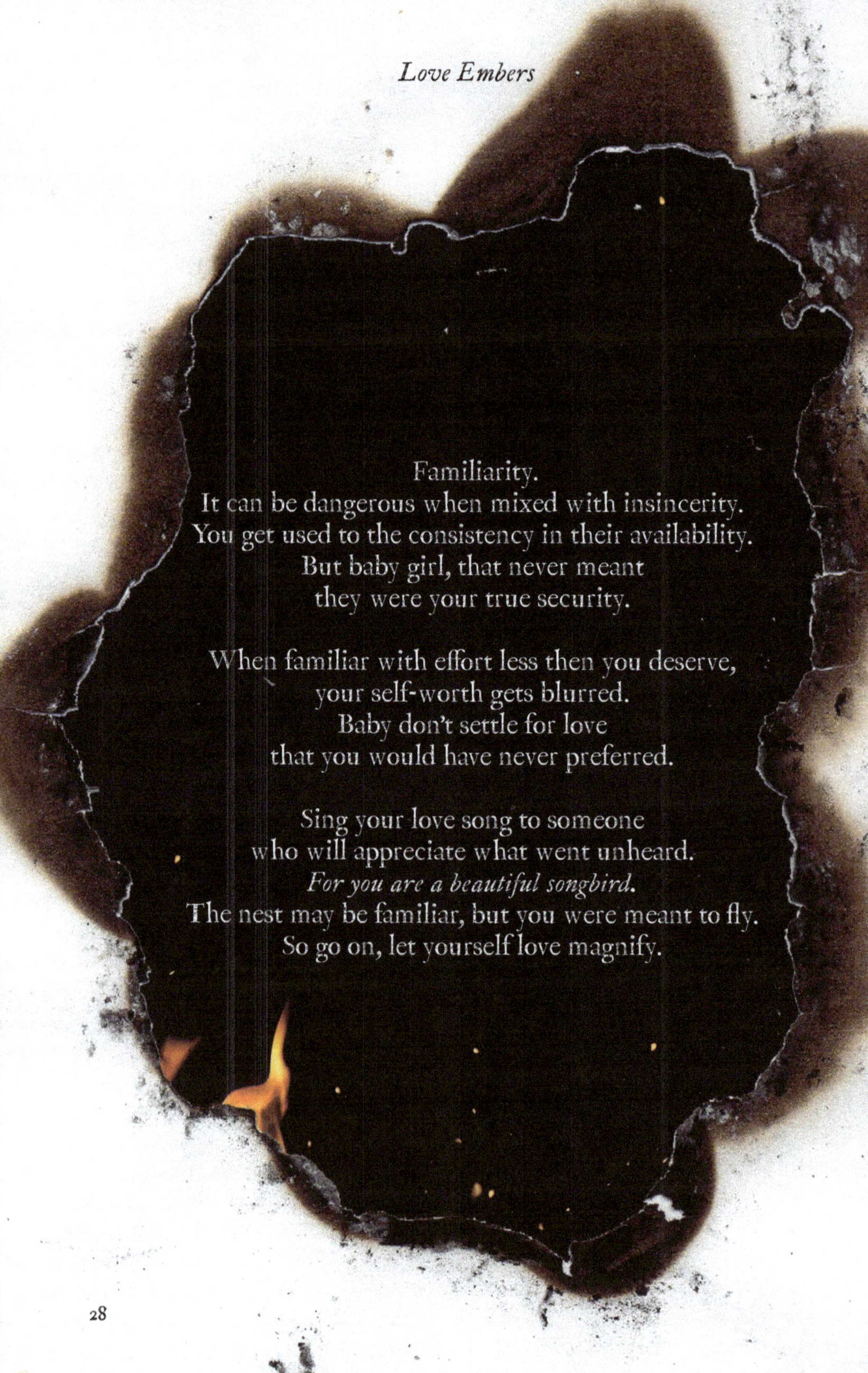

Familiarity.
It can be dangerous when mixed with insincerity.
You get used to the consistency in their availability.
But baby girl, that never meant
they were your true security.

When familiar with effort less then you deserve,
your self-worth gets blurred.
Baby don't settle for love
that you would have never preferred.

Sing your love song to someone
who will appreciate what went unheard.
For you are a beautiful songbird.
The nest may be familiar, but you were meant to fly.
So go on, let yourself love magnify.

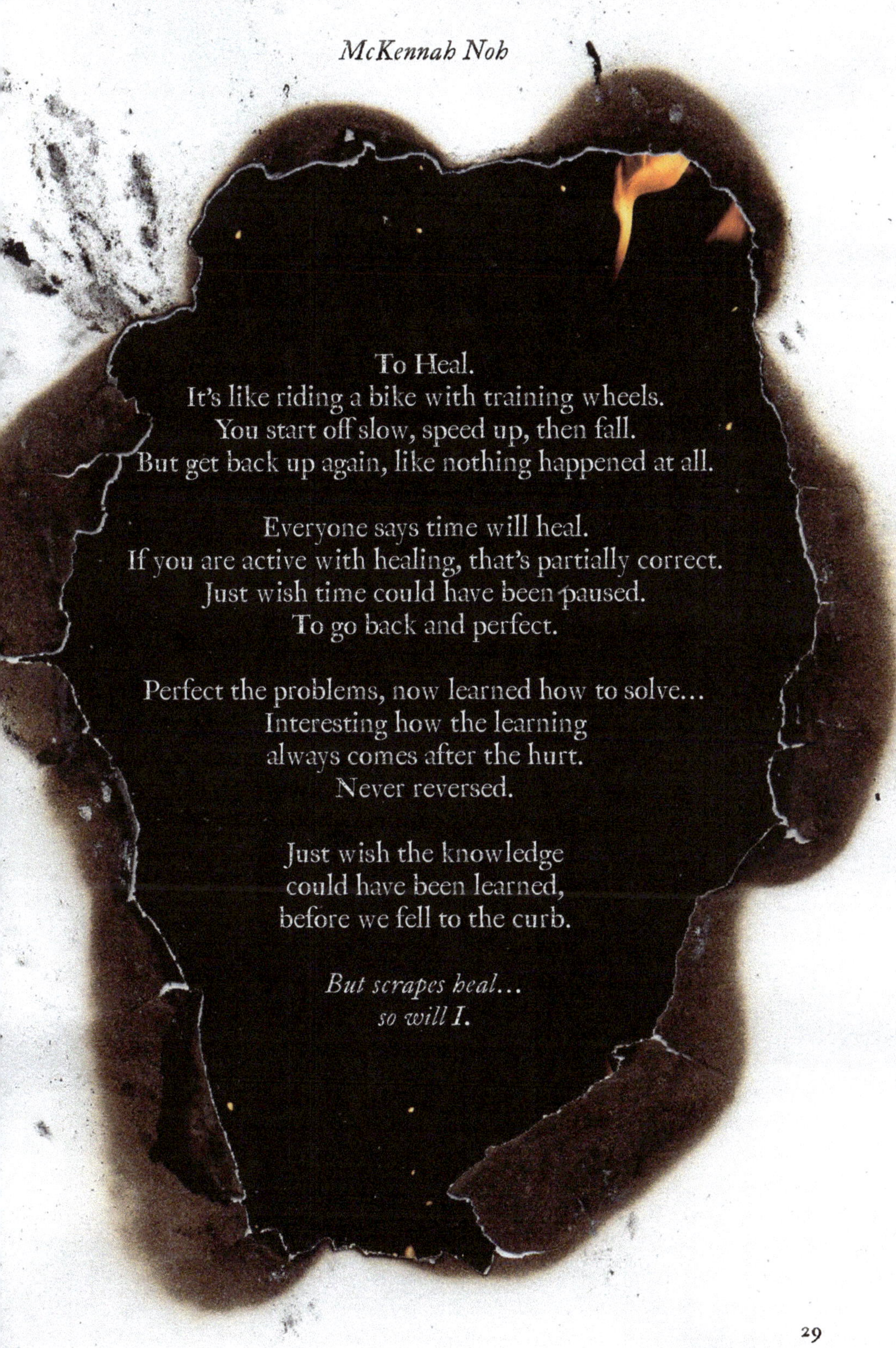
To Heal.
It's like riding a bike with training wheels.
You start off slow, speed up, then fall.
But get back up again, like nothing happened at all.

Everyone says time will heal.
If you are active with healing, that's partially correct.
Just wish time could have been paused.
To go back and perfect.

Perfect the problems, now learned how to solve…
Interesting how the learning
always comes after the hurt.
Never reversed.

Just wish the knowledge
could have been learned,
before we fell to the curb.

But scrapes heal…
so will I.

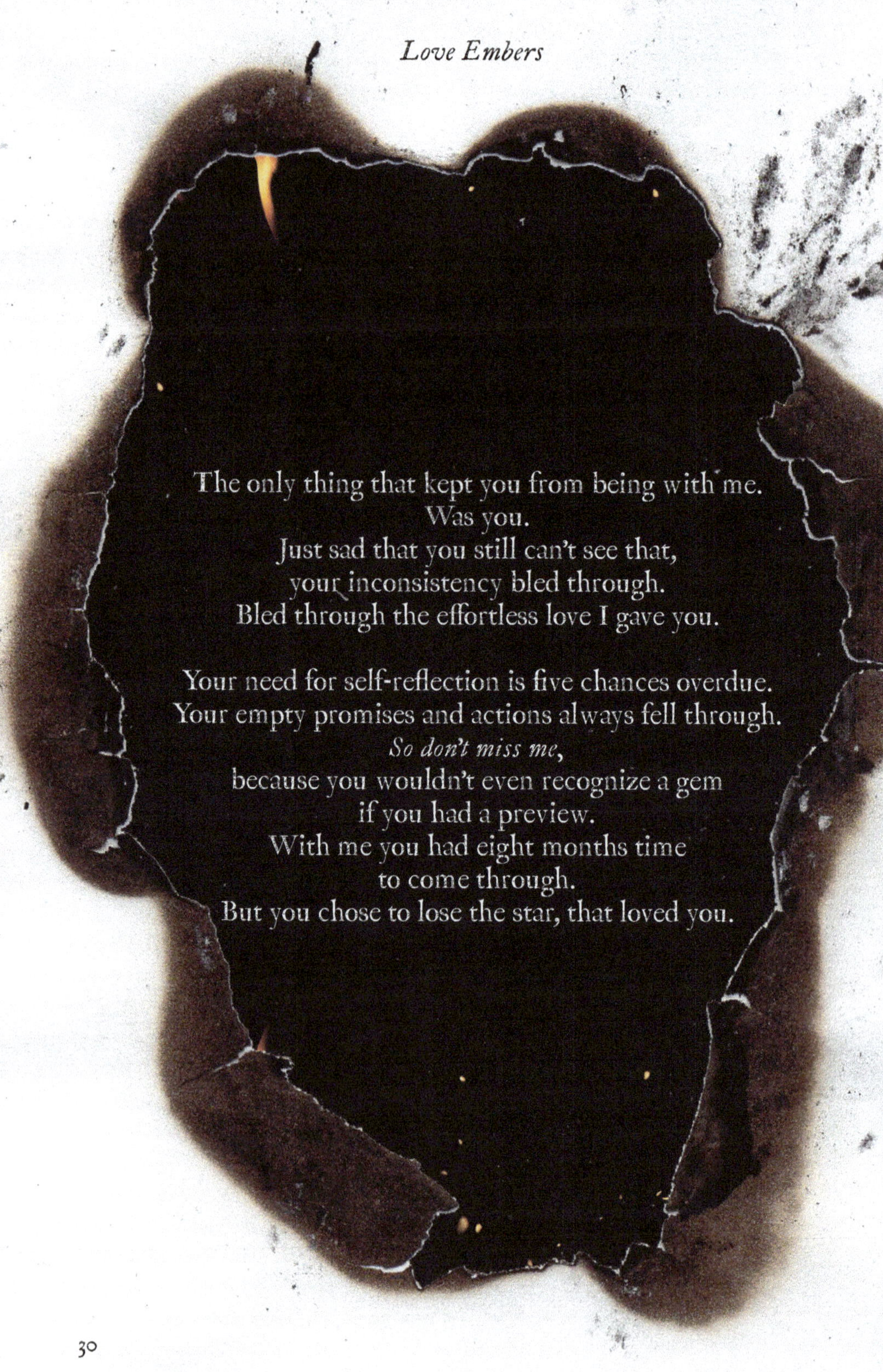

The only thing that kept you from being with me.
Was you.
Just sad that you still can't see that,
your inconsistency bled through.
Bled through the effortless love I gave you.

Your need for self-reflection is five chances overdue.
Your empty promises and actions always fell through.
So don't miss me,
because you wouldn't even recognize a gem
if you had a preview.
With me you had eight months time
to come through.
But you chose to lose the star, that loved you.

Don't go back because it's familiar or comfortable.
You already gave them your time to be vulnerable.
So just listen to the signs, don't ignore the intolerable.
They took you for granted.
Stop giving them your time, they had their chance.
Let them lay in the weeds that they planted.
You have bigger, better plans to be granted.

Lost in the woods, she searched for it.
That was her fault all along.
She settled for little berries along her way
that promised her a taste so strong.

They'd be sweet at first
but linger with bitterness and distaste.
Yet, she kept searching for the perfect embrace.

She yearned for a fruit so sweet and pure.
A fruit that would cherish her heartbeat and take care of her.
As she hunted, she got more discouraged.
For the berries she wandered upon
would leave her malnourished.

Then finally one day
she picked the most beautiful fruit.
It healed her from the scars of the rattlesnake root.
She would never settle again,
for there was no excuse.

McKennah Noh

She feels with rawness of sweet honey.
Sometimes the world doesn't know how
to handle a heart so lovely.

Leaving her to cyclical recovery.
She tries to smile though, so others days stay sunny.
Despite her emotions on her sleeves,
nobody stays, they just leave.

Leave her to pick up the pieces
that were deceived.
She's pure, and just wants to be at ease.
By those who will appreciate and receive
not leave her broken and displeased.

So as she sinks back
into the comforting seats
of her Cadillac.

She listens to the soundtrack
of her bounce back.

We sparked too fast...
No wonder it didn't last.

Her eyes will have you frozen.
Stimulated in her tidal oceans.

She'll pull you in, implosion.
Falling deeper and deeper; slow motion.

See her love's dangerous, unspoken.
She'll leave you in mystery in a moment.
Her roses so sweet, so potent.

She'll have you composing a future of devotion.
Handwoven.
Lost in her stimulation of emotion.

Chaotic
You always had me second guessing my own logic.

Your back and forth notions,
leaving me nostalgic.

Your love slowly turned into a narcotic,
leaving me numb and psychotic.

You were my favorite photograph.
When I pause to look back,
I can still see all the little imperfections
that I loved even in the pitch black.

You were my favorite setback,
too bad I have to reminisce now
with flashbacks.
Still though,
your scars were my favorite abstract.

"Your smiles one of a kind"
"It stands out from the rest, it shines"
Little did they know
she's never liked her smiles design.

Not even sometimes.
It's always the happiest people that wear the best disguise.
Because if a smile is what keeps others energized,
who is she to minimize,
the very thing that creates other soul's smile lines.

So she'll just lie…
and reply
"I like to smile, sometimes"

McKennah Noh

Pinky promise.
Pinky promise that you're different.
That your words will bring deliverance.

That your hope for us is of true significance.
So pinky promise.
Promise that you'll actually stay.
Not just say it at the convenience of a romantic date.

Please just please don't exaggerate.
The way you think you can compensate,
for the ones who only loved me to simulate,
what it be like to separate.

So please pinky promise that you'll appreciate,
the authentic beat of my heart rate.
I want a partner that will communicate,
not run me tired in figure eights.

So please pinky promise me,
because I just want to love my soulmate.
And I still believe
a pinky promise can always go a long way.

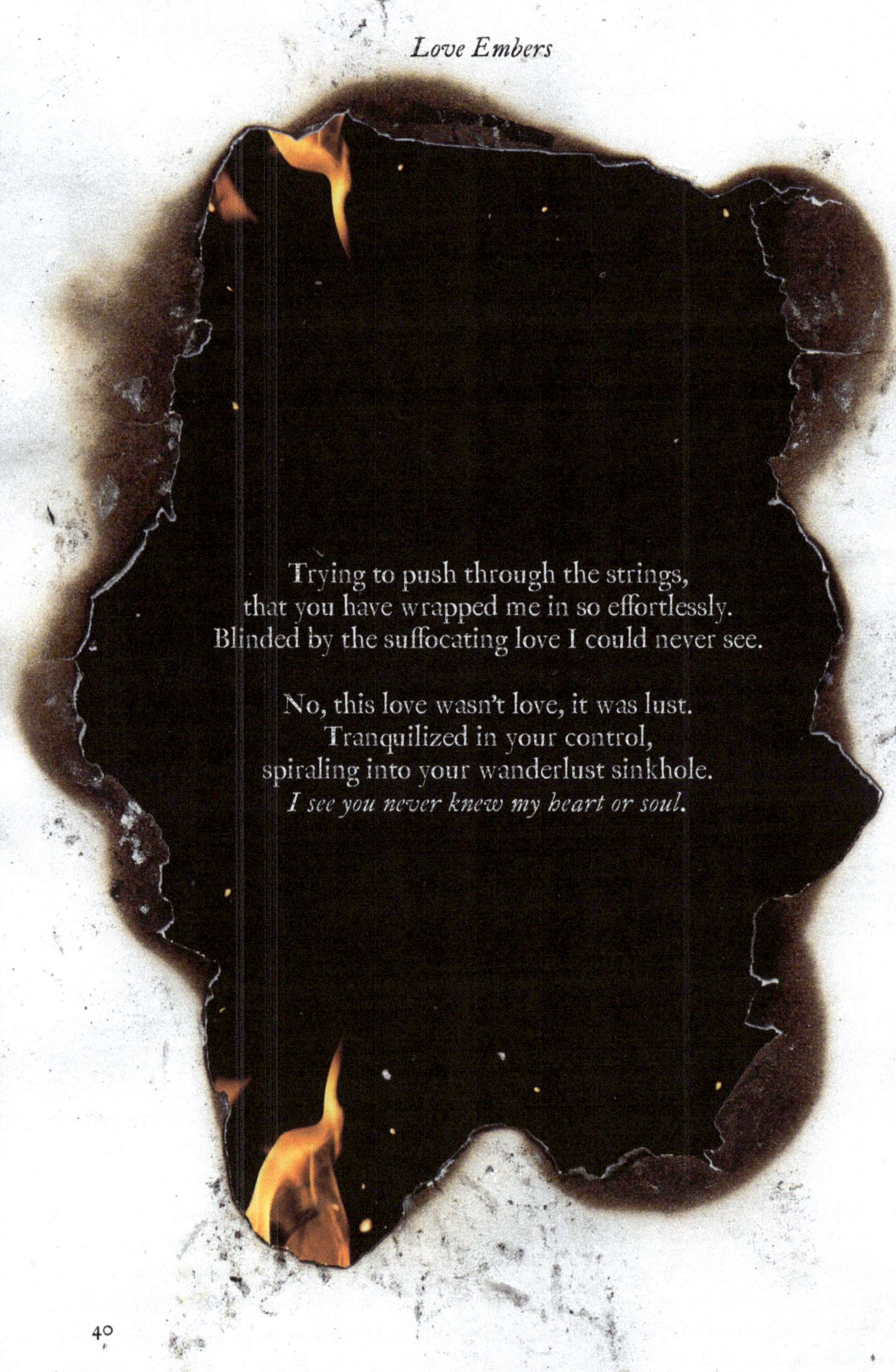

Trying to push through the strings,
that you have wrapped me in so effortlessly.
Blinded by the suffocating love I could never see.

No, this love wasn't love, it was lust.
Tranquilized in your control,
spiraling into your wanderlust sinkhole.
I see you never knew my heart or soul.

Inertia

*"You're not going forward,
but you're not going backwards.
You're just kinda there."*

I'm a bad liar…
I tell myself I'm unaffected but
you left my heart in open fire.
The days have been easier since the months prior.
Still, you seem to creep inside my mind,
making my airways tighter.

Still, I'm a bad liar…
Telling my worried friends what I felt for you is expired,
knowing every bone in my body can't hate you
let alone stop loving who used to be my highflier.

The positives I guess is the tears I shed for you have become dryer.
Your mom still checks up on me,
like how someone checks up on a campfire,
making sure the flame never goes out.
I can't lie and say I'm glad it's not you,
seeing you want to check up on me,
would be nice even a simple
"how are you" …
But what I guess hurts the most is,
even though you said you would never want this…
you allowed it to happen
with bliss.

I thought you meant it
when you said you'd never quit.
That you were "different"
and that you knew I was "worth it".
I'd be lying if I said
I hate how you made me care so much,
about you, about us,
whatever you tricked me into committing.
But fuck! I'm sick of it.
Sick of convincing myself I didn't lose, "you lost me".

But fuck, why couldn't you just see!
See how much I loved what our future could be.
See how much you meant to me.
See that all I wanted to do was grow our family tree.

Why was I never good enough for you?
Even when you'd tell me I was the first
and the last love you'd ever stick to.
I feel so stupid that I believed you.
Because you're probably fine, and
in pursuit of someone new.

Yet, I love the irony of us two,
that after everything
I'm the one still thinking of you.
Still wishing you the best
as I carry through.

I wish I knew what I actually mean to you,
but I know I'll never hear your point of view,
because you let me go…
You probably still don't understand
what you put me through.
Left me to clean up your stone-cold residue.
But alas, what to do?
It's not like you're ever thinking of me out the blue,
otherwise you would have reached out
or at least asked "how are you?"

I will say, you got me good.
Usually I know when I'm being lied to,
so funny, good one, you had me in déjà vu.
Just sucks that I had to lose you to find my value.
Amazes me how you picked trash and shallow,
over a rose gold piano.
That was ready to play
the most beautiful symphony love soprano.

Still, I'm a bad liar
with a wish that they could forget
about what they once desired.
Just praying that their thoughts
would cease- fire,
and that their heart will heal
from your venom,
black widow spider.

McKennah Noh

It's not the pain that hurt you.
It's that it was caused by the person
you least expected it to.

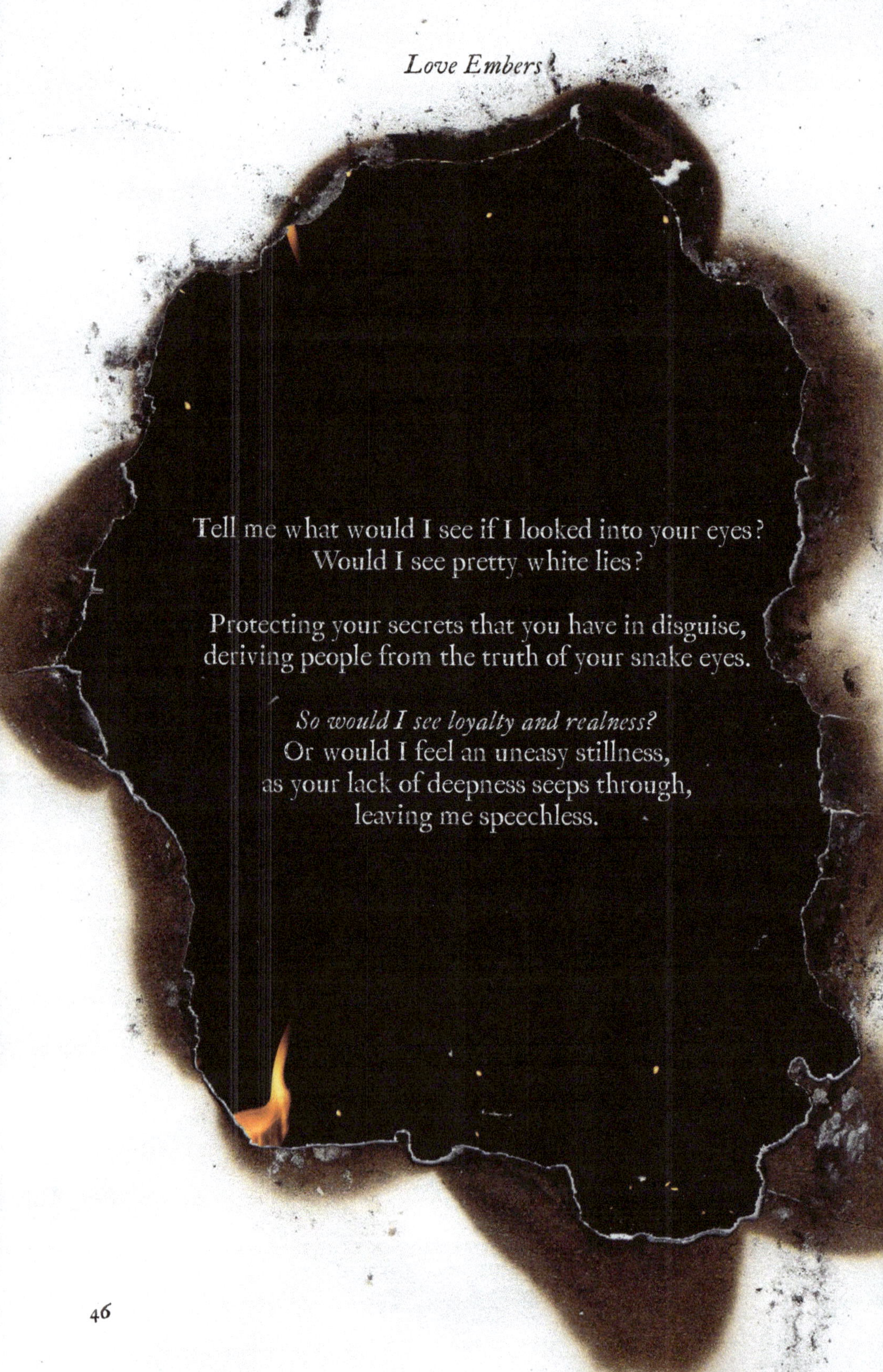

Tell me what would I see if I looked into your eyes?
Would I see pretty white lies?

Protecting your secrets that you have in disguise,
deriving people from the truth of your snake eyes.

So would I see loyalty and realness?
Or would I feel an uneasy stillness,
as your lack of deepness seeps through,
leaving me speechless.

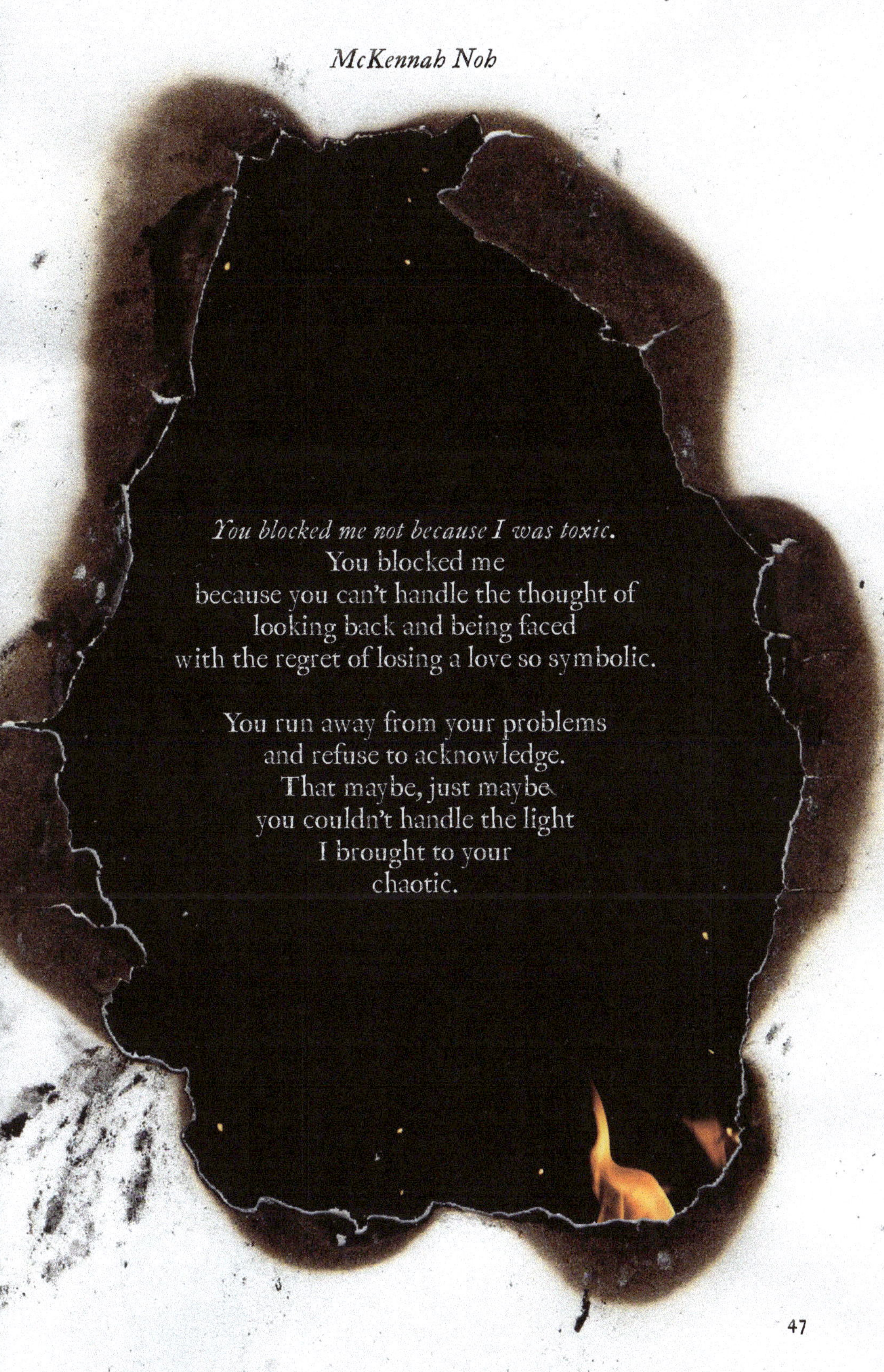
You blocked me not because I was toxic.
You blocked me
because you can't handle the thought of
looking back and being faced
with the regret of losing a love so symbolic.

You run away from your problems
and refuse to acknowledge.
That maybe, just maybe
you couldn't handle the light
I brought to your
chaotic.

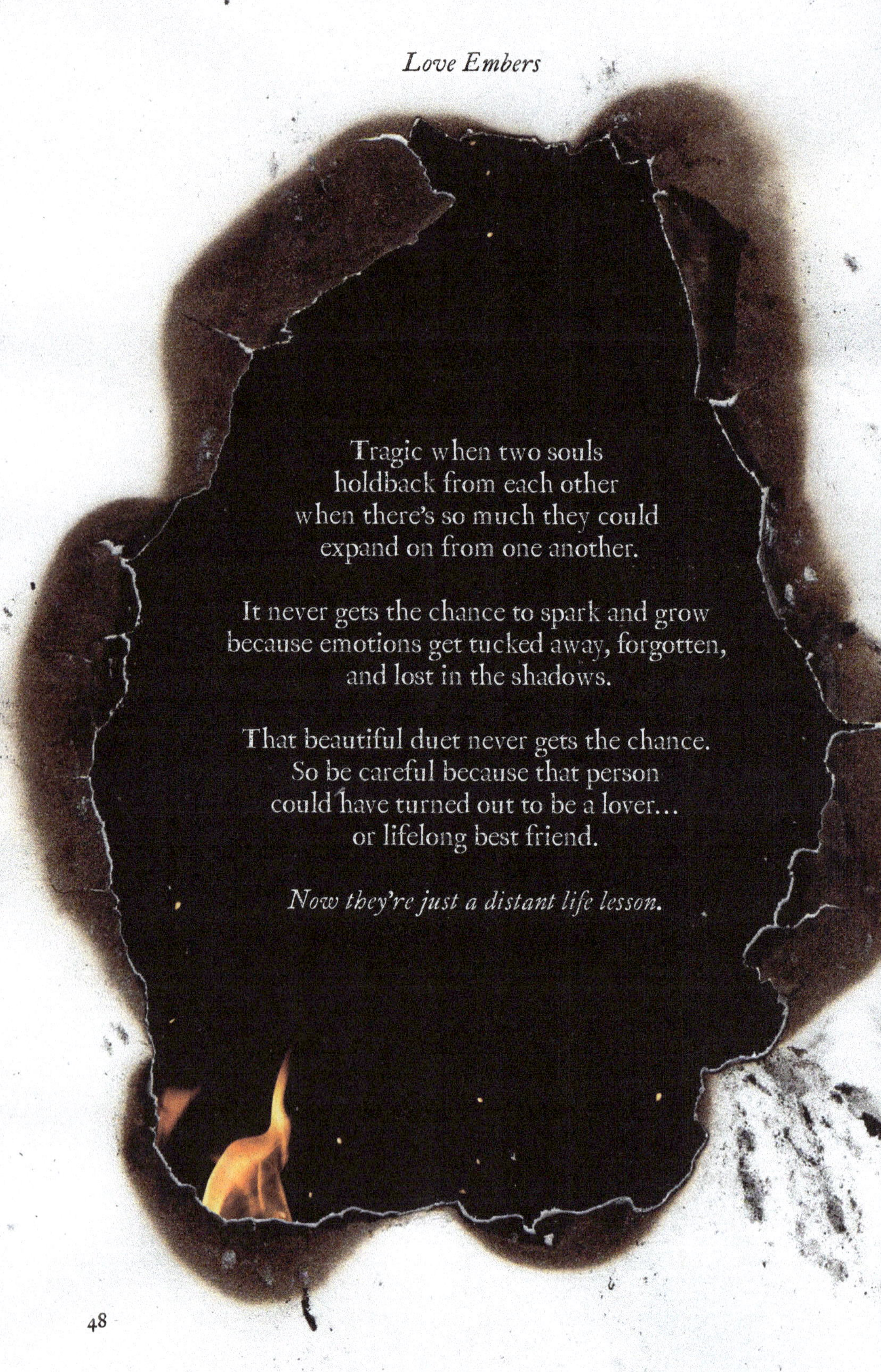

Tragic when two souls
holdback from each other
when there's so much they could
expand on from one another.

It never gets the chance to spark and grow
because emotions get tucked away, forgotten,
and lost in the shadows.

That beautiful duet never gets the chance.
So be careful because that person
could have turned out to be a lover…
or lifelong best friend.

Now they're just a distant life lesson.

She sees him but doesn't know if he sees her,
the way she wants him to.

She lights up at his smile,
wishing she could be wrapped in his presence.

He says she's been such a blessing,
yet she's still left to question.

Whether he will ever mention
his true feeling of confession.

She yearns for his affection,
he's been so different with his intentions.

She hopes he'll be a positive impression,
not just another heartbreak lesson.

She's trying to let the new come in.
She knows God has her new blessings
waiting for her to begin.

She knows she still cares for them,
but she knows it would never be the same deep within.

She has new melodies to play on her violin.
Melodies that will forgive what she will never relive.
Forgive the notes that couldn't commit.

She feels herself submit
to the care and tempo
of a new love she can't resist.

All I know is
when you close your eyes.
I have a hunch
a part of you
will still ache for the
parts of me
you can't touch
when you open them.

Even if you fall
in love with someone,
that still doesn't mean
they'll choose you.

I can tell that you're falling.
At first, I thought I was the only one.

As times gone on though, you have seen
that I'm not just anyone.
I'm a someone who stands out from everyone.

It scared me at first to notice
what you're starting to mean to me...
Falling with someone doesn't always have a guarantee,
that they'll catch you when you both disagree.

But now I see that you might be falling faster than me.
Parts of me are weary,
I don't know if we'd last in reality.
Don't know if you'd love all the parts of me.
No one's ever stuck around to see.

Is my heart ready to dive into the unseen?
There's always the chance that my heart will bleed.
I want things to be different this time
and not move with speed.
The best things take time,
I hope we both would agree.

Just please.
Be gentle with me.

I—
I don't know what this feeling is.
It's silent.
It creeps up on you
when your thoughts are quiet,
first a whisper that grows louder and louder
as it rustles through your peace.

Affectionate tension flows through my arm
into my fingertips, especially my thumb.
It makes sure to kiss my hand like a gentleman.
Leaving a pulsing charge of adrenaline that's unsettling.

It doesn't happen often,
but when it does, I know it's my body shouting caution.
Step carefully, your thoughts are slipping into waters
that will leave you in exhaustion.

Why does this still affect my mental?
Not entirely, but fragmental. Just enough
to where my body reacts to your leftover vessel.

At least I know now that this feeling
wasn't prompted by me.
It's a way my body alerts me of toxicity.

With you,
It engulfed you brilliantly.

"Come my direction."
You said as your sweet smile of demise
invited my kind eyes.

You knew what I wanted so you decided to fit my depiction,
knowing that every part of you was misleading my vision.

I didn't need what you had.
I needed a part of me
that you had to break for me to grow back.

So, why'd you have to come and say
"I have exactly what you need"
When in reality.
You were playing a game of tease.

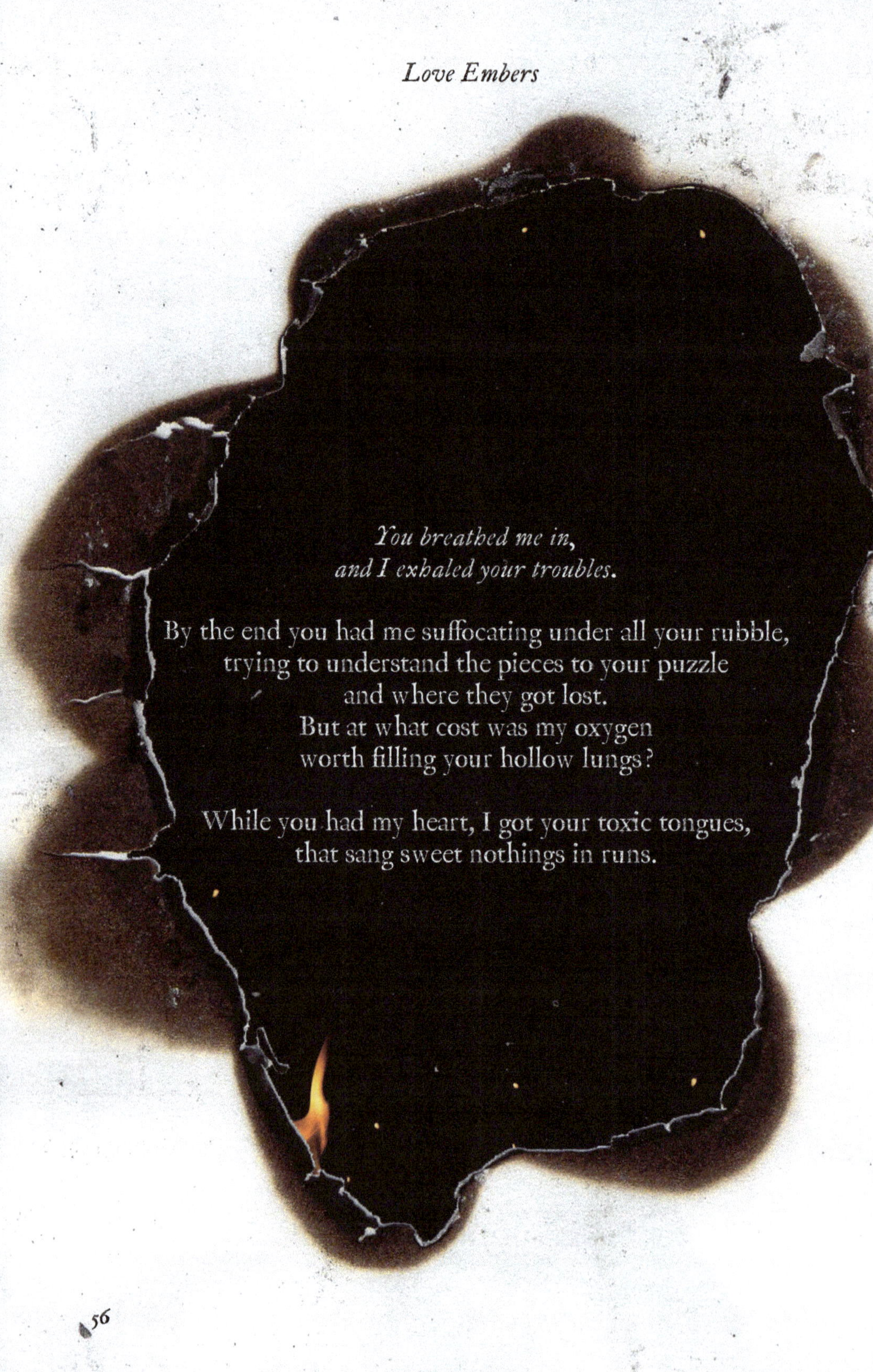

You breathed me in,
and I exhaled your troubles.

By the end you had me suffocating under all your rubble,
trying to understand the pieces to your puzzle
and where they got lost.
But at what cost was my oxygen
worth filling your hollow lungs?

While you had my heart, I got your toxic tongues,
that sang sweet nothings in runs.

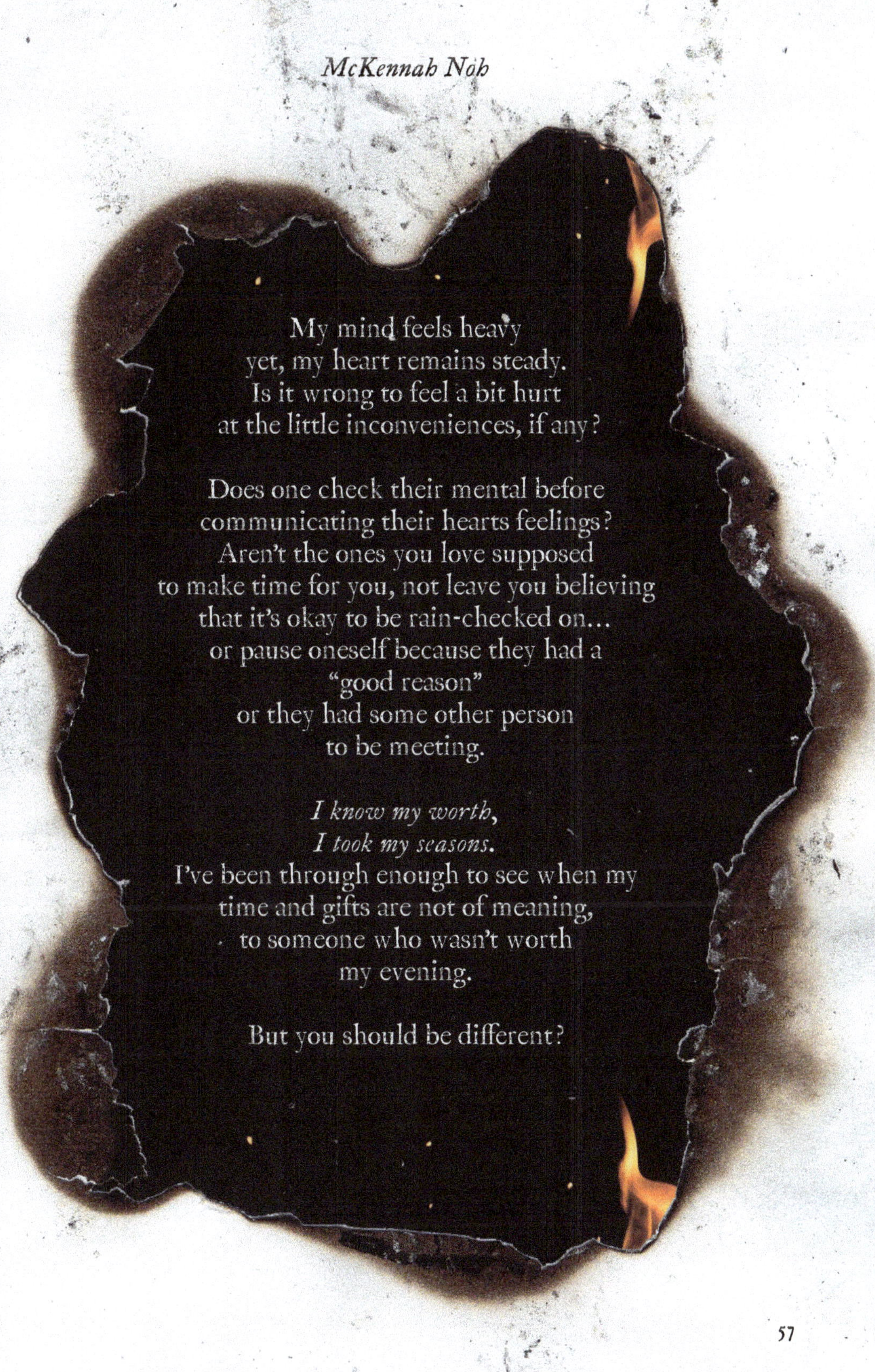

My mind feels heavy
yet, my heart remains steady.
Is it wrong to feel a bit hurt
at the little inconveniences, if any?

Does one check their mental before
communicating their hearts feelings?
Aren't the ones you love supposed
to make time for you, not leave you believing
that it's okay to be rain-checked on…
or pause oneself because they had a
"good reason"
or they had some other person
to be meeting.

I know my worth,
I took my seasons.
I've been through enough to see when my
time and gifts are not of meaning,
to someone who wasn't worth
my evening.

But you should be different?

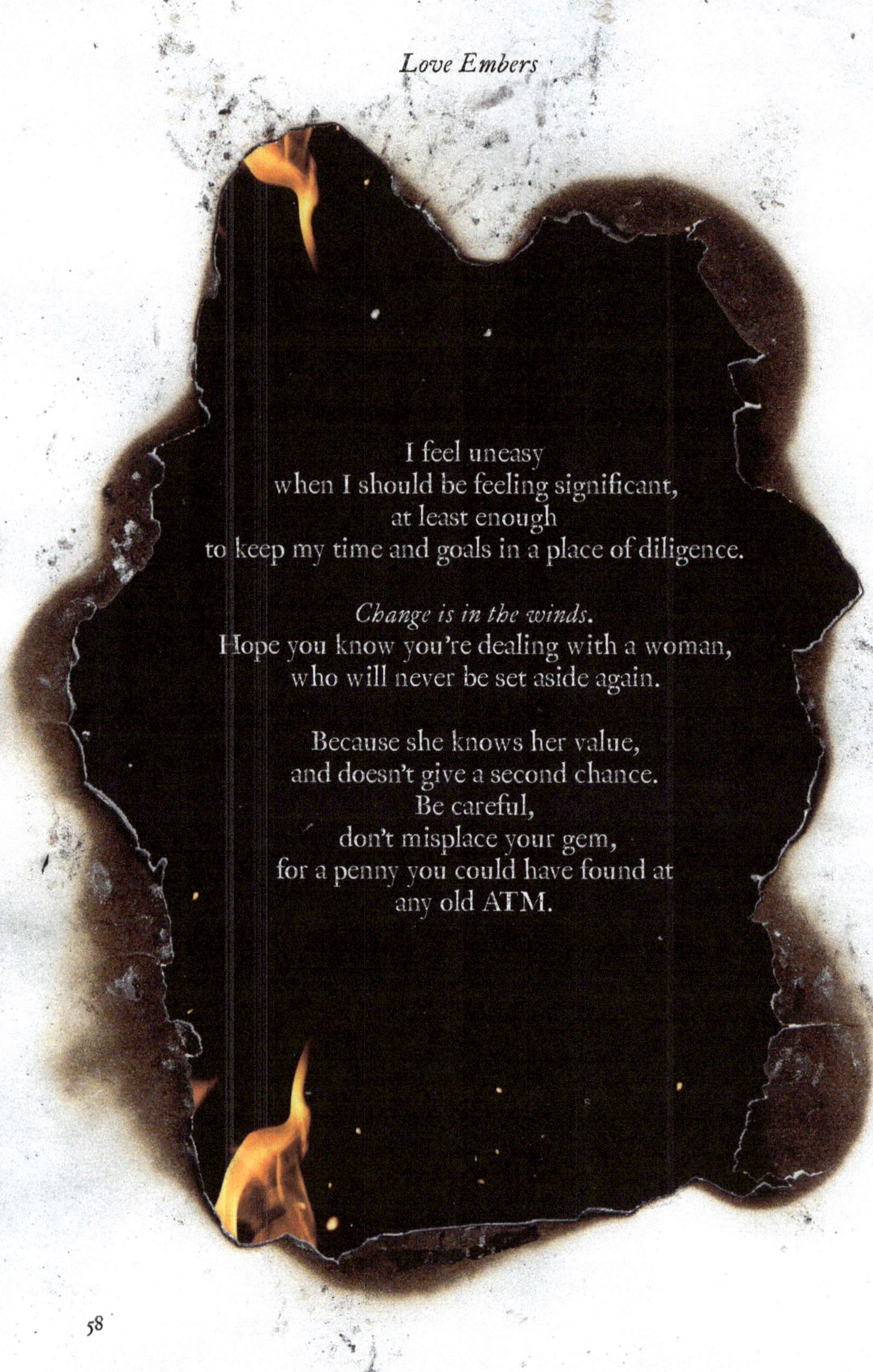
I feel uneasy
when I should be feeling significant,
at least enough
to keep my time and goals in a place of diligence.

Change is in the winds.
Hope you know you're dealing with a woman,
who will never be set aside again.

Because she knows her value,
and doesn't give a second chance.
Be careful,
don't misplace your gem,
for a penny you could have found at
any old ATM.

Shifted Kindles

Her beauty will have you tongue tied.
Scrambling for words in the riptides.
Her eyes speak volumes.
Within the corner of her smile lines,
you can see the pain where someone tossed her to the wayside.

Yet, her smile still shines,
never dulling but intensified.
She's the rarest of the rare,
you're lucky if she brings you along for the ride.

Love Embers

Sometimes when we go to pick a book off the shelf,
we look for the pretty covers.
Same with how society tends to pick their lovers.

Everyone loves the happy ending,
but no one stops to pause to read the in-between.

They just think that love is this illusion they see on the movie screens.
If you were asked the definition of love,
would you even know what it means?

No, because no one thinks about the wear and tear.
You see, love is like glassware.
Take care of it and it will remain clear.
Otherwise it turns into a shattered nightmare.

So read beyond the title of a book,
you wouldn't want to miss out on the bestseller
you didn't give a second look.

Thank you for showing me your true colors.
I almost wasted my time
trying to paint you visions of lover wonders.
A picture filled with beautiful watercolors.

But you limit yourself to one shade.
Your lack of vision was making my colors fade.

So as you watch me grow from your window shade,
hope you feel the effects of your diluted paints.
Just know, you lost your shot with an upgrade.

Your hysteria.
You send peoples energy to a frenzy within an area.
You spread like wildfire,
sparking flames between the wires.
The type of love you give will never expire.

Your energy has no room for liars.
The truth in your love takes me higher and higher.
Your love is a magnifier.
Be explicit with who you let into your empire.
Because you're a survivor,
Never lower your standards of what is required.
Always be your own admirer.

I know one day it'll hit you.
But it'll be too late for you to glue back the
pieces of us you once knew.

Because I've grown to love the better version of me,
that you'll never have the privilege to talk to.

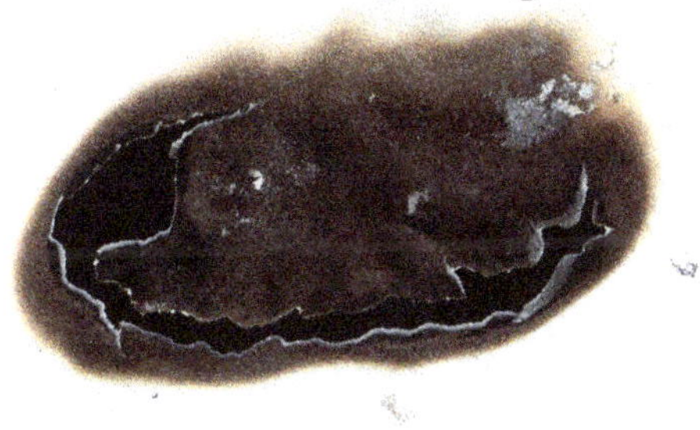

Love Embers

As she sat alone, she sank into her car
seats that hugged her curves.
She felt a sense of peace that settled her nerves.

The sky was cloaked with shades
of rich grays and blues.
Settling the evening in a calming interlude,
yet her heart still felt confused.

The trees swayed and danced in the wind.
She smiled, at their blooming grins.
But in the gentle cross winds,
she could still see old feelings in her reflection,
that have gone untrimmed.

But it's spring now.
Time to let the old leaves fall down.
Because she's realized new ones are a sprout.

Why would she want to stunt the new
found growth she's found.
No, now she knows never to drop her crown.

Two rhythms,
yet they have one heartbeat.

They dance intermittently,
in unison to a love soliloquy.

Over leaps and bounds
they grow with fluidity.

You see true love is resiliency.
Pushing through the ridged spaces,
to a place of placidity.

True love is simplicity.
Envy, distrust, and lust
won't get you to infinity.

When I first saw you, I was home.
Our love's not something
that can be captured in a poem,
but I'll try.

In your eyes, I saw our future.
I saw a soul of a genuine lover.
Someone who's heart is one of sweet clover,
who doesn't stop till their lover's cup is spilt over.

I saw a love that would last till we're older.
Growing closer and closer,
shoulder to shoulder.

She's an
old soul
trapped
in a world
of the
superficial.

"*What's your type*"
As he looked at me with anticipation.
With hopes that he would match my definition.
Hoping he would break my trend of repetition.

I simply replied
"*Someone who's my best friend, with kind eyes,*
who will mean when they say they love me
and can empathize"

McKennah Noh

You had me sitting around waiting
for something that wasn't in your DNA.

My type of love language was a distant foreign trade.
To the common misconception
of your generations love clichés.

From a glance I would have missed you.
Missed out on a connection that I'm not used to.

So, I'm glad that I took a second glance.
Blessed that you felt comfortable enough to open up to me,
you took a chance.
A chance that felt so natural, the risk factor
of falling didn't even seem to scare us given the
sudden circumstance.
A circumstance that will possibly bud into romance.
One can only hope.
My heart feels like it's just received a surprised letter,
concealed in a tender envelope.

McKennah Noh

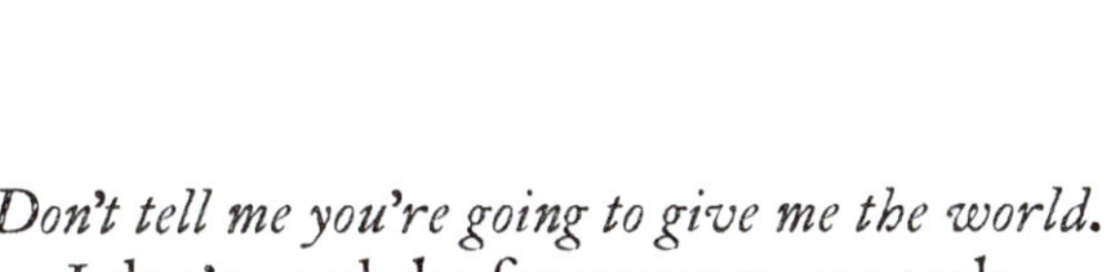

Don't tell me you're going to give me the world.
I don't need the fancy roses or pearls.
You're dealing with a simple girl.

Tell me you'll add to my world.
Push me to be better, not just some showgirl.
Don't tell me pretty lies when you say this is forever.
Because true devoted love takes effort.

True love doesn't run at the first tremor,
it sticks around through the displeasure.
So tell me your willing to remember,
all the promises you said today,
when there was no pressure.

What lies beneath is what the wandering eye never pauses to see.
Behind the alluring patterns and charming depiction
lies the actuality.

Behind the strings of the canvas,
lays the madness.
But at surface level, the shades of sadness vanish.
Till all that's left to admire are the fake portraits
that are secretly damaged.

So here is your challenge, look beyond the canvas.
Truly examine.
Before you're just another art critic
that has taken advantage.

The love I crave is flexible.
It doesn't require any decimal.

The love I crave is fixable.
Requiring two partners to be respectable.

The love I crave is unforgettable,
it'll have the perfect balance between obsessional and incredible.

I crave a love so collectible.
So rare, so beautiful, so plentiful.

A gratifying love that values the sentimental
over the preferable skeptical of the sexual.

Love Embers

Wrapped up in my sweater,
they smile back at me with sweet forever eyes.

Painting scarlet blue skies,
giving me butterflies…
Every time they sneak up from behind
pulling my waist closer to theirs.

They make me want to sit and memorize,
every little freckle, crease, line…
that is personalized,
to the love of my life.

As I pull down their Levi's,
So we can unwind till the sunrise.
Their love has me stigmatized,
anticipating their next pulse of touch,
I finally have a love where the basics aren't asking for "too much".

— *I'm happy*

In a crisis, or even epidemic,
you see who truly valued you like a relic.

Who truly saw your authentic,
not just your aesthetic

You see real colors through the hectic.
Suddenly, the people who slept on you want to give you all the credit.

Keep your last-minute love,
I got my real ones up in heaven.

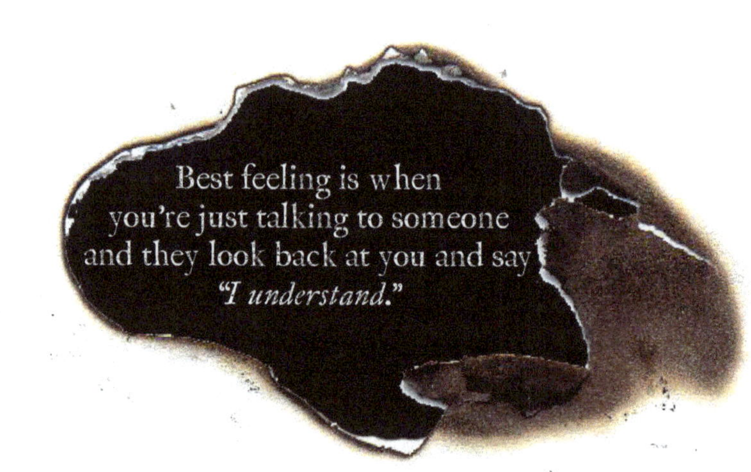
Best feeling is when
you're just talking to someone
and they look back at you and say
"I understand."

Love me slow and sweet, baby.
Love me to the beats of my heart's melodies.

Love me recklessly with loyalty.
Love listening to the patterns of my soul's variety,
block out the cliché pressures of society.

Love me joyfully.
Embrace my child heart innocence
but take me seriously.

For I am a growing flower.
A powerful.
Rare.
Delicacy.

Are we just friends?
The way you look at me seems to blend,
into the vision of a romanticized lens.

Our conversations always turning into memorable gems.
Our differences beautifully cleanse
the scars we both discuss from our past trends
that we have now put to an end.

With every warm hug, and little remark though,
I see myself falling into your tempo.
Even my friends have noticed a new afterglow
that I now see in me since I've let the past go.

You're a personality I feel that I've met a long time ago.
We flow so naturally like wind blowing through the limbs
of a weeping willow.
Peaceful.
Easy.
Our connection's not too needy, but dreamy.
It has no restrictions, we feel freely.
You caught me off guard,
it's like you get me completely.
How freaky.
I hope we know what we're doing,
because feelings can be sneaky.

McKennah Noh

The words we speak,
are rooted deeper than we think.

Some say the key to one's soul are the eyes,
but I challenge to say otherwise.

The key to one's soul is the words,
for their words are connected to their heart cords.

*Each word they speak
shows their true colors underneath.*

Be wary of those who speak of others,
you will be next even if you are close as brothers.

So listen closely to the words.
They'll help guide you towards
the right people who will uplift and support.
Instead of the snakes who spread their venom for sport.

I've been pushed out of my comfort zone.
To new parts of me I never knew I owned.

I was never alone,
I was just around the wrong people that shook my foundation stone.

But now I've grown,
feels so good to see new sights I flew to on my own.

With wisdom and love let alone,
I have continued on to new stepping stones.

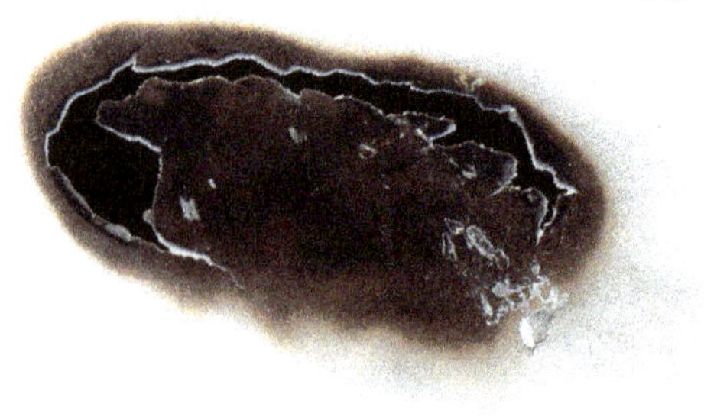

Be the person she looks for in a crowded room.
Be the person that helps her bloom.
Be the person that takes her out to a dining room,
not just someone who sees her in the bedroom.

Be a love that supports and doesn't assume.
Be a love that doesn't confuse or abuse.
Instead help her improve,
taking her to higher aptitudes.

Be a love that executes,
Not a love full of excuses.
Be her muse.
Feed her soul, like sweet apple juice.
Be someone she could never refuse.
Be someone she could never substitute.
Be a love you'd want to love you.

Let them keep guessing.
She's a mystery story worth telling.

Her spirit of the moon is so refreshing.
Yet perplexing,
Because she gives you enough
to pull you in with tides so caressing.
Then leaves you tongue tied, begging.
Begging for her to reveal more than she is letting.

Every inch of her will not be what you're expecting.
For a beautiful crescent moon has more light to it
than it's projecting.

McKennah Noh

that builds the satisfaction of the embrace.

It is the poker face that sews the threads of mystery
in love's queen annes lace.

The land of the unknown provides a hiding place,
for emotions to lay quite just incase
things don't go as planned when brought face to face.

But oh, how the tensions build like the flames of a fireplace.
Steaming flames dancing with embers that beautifully interlace.

The thriller of subtlety,
that throws two hearts into a master puzzle,
both scrambling to finish it piece by piece.

In hopes that their newfound discovery,
will be worth the perplexity
of their captive emotions
held by
mystery.

Love Embers

"You're my unexpected"
"You're my unknown"
"I don't have to put thought to the feeling that I have with you"
"As the days go on, it gets better and better when you're involved"

"She's radiant love,
a vulnerability so graceful it reflects true love."

"It's a feeling past lust"
"She's my best friend"

People have come so accustomed to the fake.
No wonder the real seem to be taken for disbelief.

The fake have subdued to the outbreak,
of superficial love intake.

The "love" that is filled with temporary promises of wedding cake,
then bittersweet realities of heartbreak.

It's unfortunate the real are the ones who are left betrayed.
Left stranded on the curb of the fast lane,
wishing that people wouldn't take advantage of their rare heartbeat.

Is there an escape?
An escape that lasts longer than a holiday.
All the real can hope is someday.
Someday the fake will stop and see how they manipulate.
And see that all along,
they were the ones losing in life's card game.

The fake wonder why they constantly feel unsafe,
It's because they push away anything real and true that could help
them not be afraid.
For the real…
I caution to reevaluate your landscape.
In the tall grass can be indigo snakes,
waiting to feed your pure soul the enemy's sweet cakes.

I don't understand why we go in these cycles.
Every time I think we are growing,
you hit me with a downward spiral.

You make me cling to my Bible,
hoping that one day God will forgive your toxic recitals.

It hurts me how fast you spit your venom.
Your moods and personalities seem to blend into a twisted welcome.
I fear you're drifting more and more away from heaven,
but you don't listen to me...
you object lights direction.

Why are you filled with so much aggression?
Don't you see what it's done to your life's progression?

It's left all your relationships in question.
You don't even realize how deep your words cut through people's skin,
everlasting impression.

Every day I can just see the real pain behind your facial expression,
and even though you've hurt me I still pray for you to be forgiven.

I hope one day you start to pay attention,
to the damage you've caused,
seen in your own reflection.

I hope one day you make the effort towards correction.
Take appreciation to people's suggestion,
and see through new perceptions.

Just please wake up,
want you to see you at the tree of heaven.

When I think I've finally forgotten all the shadows
you've left in my mind.
The sun reflects in the rooms where your memories
are still left behind...
Leaving me quarantined in this clouded frame of mind.
Asking the moon why?

Why do I feel like during the time I was the problem?

That held back bonds that now are in blossom.
Feeling stupid that while your memory still lingers in my mind,
in yours, mine is forgotten.
Things hit different when you see them smiling,
with the same people they used to tell you were
lying, hiding, and striking.
Then, I tell myself God removed them for the better.
Removed you.
I've found new shades of worldview,
that were well past overdue.
Just wish the sun would stop bringing to light,
the past shadows of your toxic residue.

McKennah Noh

I want a love so high...
the stars get jealous.

Everyone nowadays dreams of a love like velvet.
Why can't people recognize the love we need though?

The love that's neglected in the streets of the status quo.
But Oh?
Sorry I forgot the color of one's skin
determines the weight of one's cargo.
Some carry more than others. Carrying histories scars. Jim Crow.

"All lives matter"
No, they don't.
The people decided that the day they oppressed darker tones.

So why is this the love that people have let go?
They'd rather tiptoe around trigger words than change histories tempo.

How many new hashtags must die and go,
for there to be justice for all these lost souls?

Instead of investing in a new patio,
how about investing in organizations that will change tomorrow.
This so-called "growth" has been a never ending pattern. Staccato.

Slight changes, but then a bullet shifts us back to the game show.
Game show our "united nation" calls freedom.
Even though one man could live while the other is beaten.
Oh, and for no reason.
Only probable cause that was needed,
was that this man was born into a world of treason.

Love is what this world is begging to be given.
Waiting for the day a freeman...
has his
freedom.

Your mouth moves just as senseless as your conscious.
Constantly painting false masterpieces to help your subconscious.
You say you want "us"
Then take every chance you get to break your promise.
Yeah, I've heard it all,
I'm your "flawless goddess"
yet all I receive is your dishonest vomit.
You build up my expectations only to demolish.

Broken glass can never be polished.
So I'm done, if I'm going to be honest.

McKennah Noh

The feelings flooded first,
before my thoughts could repair the holes
of which they rushed through.

It's like with every touch, you knew how to breakthrough.
Knew how to undo all the rooted scars within
my tissue.

So, I'll continue to thank you
with the only ways I know how to.
Being there and continuing to get to know you.

All the parts that you usually don't let seep through,
I see clearly from our body's sensual residue.
Fascinating how we can tell what the other's feeling
without the need of an interview.

Your eye's always spinning records of "I love you".
Oh and, just a secret between me and you,
You're my eye's favorite person to talk to too.

"I'll love you right the first time."
Man, if I had a penny for every time I heard this line,
I'd be chillin on an island drinkin' sweet wine.

So, baby just go the other way,
I'm over here praying for something for a better day.
For someone that won't waste my time or play,
and treat me the way the wind caresses
a wind chime on a Sunday.

I want someone who doesn't just love me in their downtime.
My standards stay at full-time,
sorry not sorry my love's too warm for your wintertime.

Not my fault you can't keep up with my nursery rhymes.
But in the meantime,
Why don't you find someone else
that'll believe

I don't need you.
I found me.
So you really have the audacity to push
yourself onto me?

No.
Not in my reality.
See I have my own PhD.
I've learned red flags I refuse to oversee.

True partners work every day to deserve
their queen.
To lose the beautiful rarity
of her botanical serene,
would be a pain they know would haunt
them in their dreams.

So don't ever think that I'd ever need
to depend on my partner to water my mustard seeds.

God gave an empire capable of this queen.
So either support her by her side,
or watch from the screens.

Forgiving
Incense

No more games and no more pain.
I've forgiven what's done and moved on to new terrain.

How could I expect myself to grow if I still
think back to your name?

That would be the borderline definition of insane,
thinking you could change, when the outcomes would always
come out the same.

I love you though and I always will,
but I can't allow our past to distill what I'm meant to fulfill.
;
No… not anymore, because this new me
I have grown to love even more.
I love the strength, wisdom, and courage this new me stands for.

I almost allowed the memory of you to set me back therefore,
almost pulling me away from the growth I've made
like an actor falling through a trapped door.

But then I stopped and asked, what for?
What good would it do for me to sit here and think about you
when I could truly move on to seek clearer and more godly
views.

I'd never want to speak bad of you,
or anyone for that matter due to
the fact that one should love thy neighbor
like you'd want them to love you.

So no,
I will never wish you poor or ill.
I will pray for you to grow till your cup overflows.

So here's to letting new reflections in.
Here's to letting go of what could have been,
and growing towards the path where angels win.

We could have made amends.
At least stayed in each other's lives as friends.
But you have always looked through a diverging lens.

Losing your presence has turned into a cleanse.
It's still bittersweet at times but you're the one who let go of a gem.
The funniest part is, that's not the "truth: you're telling "them".
But it's okay, fools will always be condemned.

I see you drowning, and I just want to save you.
My heart aches for what you've been put through.

But to you, it's what you're used to.
Always left with no one to turn to.

If only you knew you're the person I look up to.
The only one that ever followed through.

I want to help you, but I don't know how to…
Since seven years old I've known your point of view.
Every detail of pain, worry, and anxiety you bled through.

Everyday I pray that God will save you.
Give you what's been overdue.
I hope you know I love you…

I wish you'd believe me when I say these scars are
something you will grow through.
Please see your value.
I don't want to imagine this world without you.

So I asked *"What is your type of love?"*

"Love is a question.
Love is a solution.
Love is a switch that turns on and off.
Love is beautiful.
Love is unconditional.
There's never a period.
That's what makes it unconditional."

With that you left me your sweet confessional.

You tried so hard to put up this tough bark.
So that the creatures of the night couldn't get to you in the dark.

But I saw something more.
I saw the growing internal war.
That your tough bark helped you ignore.

To me it was like looking through a screen door,
that thought it was solid.
Your limbs and fruits stayed in seasons of stolidity.
You pushed away anything that could help you grow; pollen.

You had all your voids vaulted.
Until I came and saw through your tough bark now exhausted.

But the winds of challenge and change, made you nauseous.
You always moved with caution.
Lessons never grasped, forgotten.

Leaving your internal holes to broaden.
I gave you the chance to blossom.
Instead you fed your holes with gossip.

So your hollowness is no longer my problem.
I just accepted that illusion is your common.

*I had to experience you so
I would know what to never go back to.*

Thank you for the preview,
of a love I wouldn't have gotten with you.

So now I can go on,
to find myself and someone who will push through.

I got a value too good for me,
no one has the capacity to adapt to the vision I see.

God made me his honoree.
I take in every blessing he gifts me.
Air in my lungs, a kind heart, loyalty, and my family.

Don't expect me to trip over what you couldn't see,
he didn't give me this path because I'm a weaker link.
He gives his hardest challenges to the most extraordinary.
So just sit down and watch me split the sea.
Because I not only believe.
I have the strength of the everlasting.

Thank you for giving us your light.
Even though we were born to turn away from you,
you continue to fight...

You valued us above yourself.
So we could have life and the chance to excel.
You've taught me to value myself.

The amount of gratitude overwhelms,
for you have shown me I don't need the validation of others,
I needed it from myself.

My ears are no longer trapped to the gossiping hotel.
Instead you've surrounded me with your wisdom to repel.
Repel the mockers that intentions are to dwell.
Dwell on the potential I've always had to excel.

So the highest, I thank you,
for you have shown me the truth.
The forever prevailing truth that soothes.

You've freed me from my past.
Now I can see the brighter forecast,
that you set aside, just for me to grasp.
You love your craft,
I finally see my value...
At last.

As the stars of the galaxy smiled back at her
she raised up her words to them in a whisper

For she's the towns drifter,
mystery, and luscious elixir.

Even in the darkest night,
you can always find a source of light.

There will be a tomorrow,
and new light will overflow.

A Poem to My Future Someone

I've honestly never met someone like you.

So genuine.
So caring, deep, and thoughtful.

You take the time to understand the whole me,
and every version I come with,
you welcome with open arms…

You're not quick to judge,
instead you listen and notice.
You pay attention to the details…
My smile lines…
The way my eyes crinkle at the ends.

Nobody's ever noticed,
the way you've noticed them.

Nobody's ever loved me the way you do.

Nobody's ever paid attention
to the little things that I do.

I don't think I'd want anyone else to either.

I've never been so lucky and thankful
to have a person like you in my life.

You've taught me so much,
in so little time.
You've shown me that I can still
trust my heart with someone...

I can let my guard down
and let my walls come undone.

You're the first person that's ever told me,
I'm someone they can't live without.

Usually, it's the other way around.

First person to show me
there are people
that go the extra mile,
just because they wanted to see you smile.

I still don't know how to take it all in,
I've just never been valued the same as I value them.

I love you so much I hope it's not a temporary chapter.

Either way, as long as we stay in each other's lives...
that's all that matters.

*Sometimes you have to get dragged in the dirt,
before you can see the flowers.*

To new beginnings.
To digging deeper into yourself.
To letting go.
To forgiving.
To new love.
To new adventures.
To self-love.
To finding clarity.

— *To us*

He has a way of bringing things full circle.
Bringing out the things we thought
we had forgotten in our internal.

It's weird to see yourself surrounded by people of your past,
captured in memories of old photographs.

For a second, it makes you wonder
what ever happened to those connections?
That ended up drifting to distant directions.

If anything, though I've learned the lesson,
that its okay to think back and appreciate
the ones who were meant to be reflections.

It's his way of protecting.
Protecting us from the things
that would have kept us from our future blessings.

It's his way of teaching us the power of selecting.
Selecting the ones who will uplift us instead of repressing.

McKennah Noh

Last night you touched a place deeper
than my heart.
You touched a place where my walls slowly
fell apart.

I'll admit
it caught me off guard.
Seeing myself for the first time in months subdue to
the emotions I thought
I had retired.

It's crazy how a moment can spark old wires,
make you pause and reflect what
growth is still required.

I didn't even know that silence was a fear,
more of a lingering hurt I didn't know was here.
I like how you made me rethink though,
I have more healing to do
that's distinct now.

So here's to further learning the new me,
the new me that will truly be free.
Free from the
fear of love scarcity,
because the love I now see,
will always be there for me.

Legacy.
It's not something simple that's thrown together in a recipe.
It takes integrity.

Knowing that you're living for the longevity,
not getting distracted by the enemy.

Not letting others control the beat of your melody.
If there's anything I've learned, a true masterpiece is built steadily.
A legacy is built by one who's mastered empathy.

By one who love thy neighbor breathlessly,
never hesitating to lead others to clarity.

So what will you choose to be in the midst of the world's treachery?
A simple memory lost in the ripples of other
identities.

Or an everlasting…

Legacy.

As he watched her walk past,
he knew that he'd seen his dream girl at last.

From a distance she'd never know,
the lengths and leaps head be willing to go,
so that pain is something she'd never have to know.

Everyday he'd do the little things.
Opening the door for her and letting her know that he's listening.

He had thought he had crushed before,
but with her it was something different he adored.

He barely knew her yet felt the need to be near,
felt the need to be the peace to her prayer.

It's crazy how she influenced him,
he'd catch himself
sitting up straighter,
even fixing his hair,
doing anything to make sure he was prepared.

*It was like he was stuck in a compass
with her as his true north.*

Her smile was the gravity holding his soul to earth.
She was a girl who knew her worth.
So it goes.

- love

To think I almost let you creep back into my mind.
Thankful to have the wisdom to know
that was the enemy trying to decline,
and unwind the growth that I have claimed to be mine.

I didn't lose a thing.
I was separated from your paths
to take on a vision only the great's can grasp.
A path designed for me to unclasp,
and reap in the fruits of my hard work and trials.

I thank you for your season.
If you never showed me the true colors that you were leaking,
I would have never gone on to higher dreaming and achieving.

I will no longer be caught in the cycle of infectious misleading.
You lost a gem that will never stop succeeding.

That's not on me love,
that's on your sightless sneaking.

Week in paradise.
Every breeze of ocean air is like an entice,
that pulls me closer to the light in your eyes.

With you, risk is no sacrifice,
reality stems from what is fantasized.
You make me want to sit down and recognize.
All the beautiful blessings that have come from your sunrise.
As we walk with the stars tonight.

Even in black night your warmth is my headlight.
Thank you for letting me sink into your world of
Paradise.

As she grows into the women she was meant to be,
she makes sure to pause
and hear her creator's voice through the breeze.

She may have doubts every now and so,
but his voice stays steady guiding the sails of her boat
as she pulls and sways through
the waves.

His powerful love never fails to save.
Save her from the worldly grave.

So, as she grows and pours her soul into him.
He'll lift her when she needs help to swim.
So she can continue to let his light in.

Thank you, G.

McKennah Noh

*Relationships and bonds are worth more
than a million stars.*

In each one you have a personal memoir.
Waiting to be heard like the cords of a guitar.

So sit back and take the time,
to be still and recognize.

To hold the people around you close
because at the end they're worth the most.

Blooming
Fire Flower

"I will never walk away from you again"

as she looked at her reflection.

Sing... Sing a song that is only yours,
that no one else can ignore.
Sing a song that rings truth,
that will call others back home to the fires of their youth.
Life seems to throw us these useless clichés, every time we
seem to lose our way.

But never lose sight of your own unique song,
never bend your melody to the beat of another drum; so, we sing.
Until the song of a battered wing restraints our notes.
So even if we sing all day long, all our songs are tainted,
by the pound of society's drum.

The drums whose vibrations shook through the wars of our past.
The drums that stood for "freedom at last".
But today the drums of war are heard
in our everyday grocery stores.
Heard in the broken journal writings locked away
in little Anne's chest drawers.

So sing. Sing your song of freedom and fire.
Sing what freedom truly desires.
So, what is freedom, and do we even have it,
or are our songs of
"freedom" masked by the drums of havoc?

Love Embers

She's my sugar bee.
Sweet and smooth like raw honey.

She'll leave you wanting more,
sweet as sugar cane straight to the core.

She'll have you addicted; drugstore.
She'll have you speechless,
giving you more than you could ask for.

I got it from my mama.
So don't ask me why I don't entertain
your childish drama.

I've been raised better;
my only concerns are about them commas.
If your energy is not helping me succeed,
then honey, sorry but your position's relieved.
Because mama didn't just raise me,
she raised a supreme.

Love Embers

You're mysterious,
but in a good way.

Feeling your warmth radiate,
keeps my worries at bay.

It's been awhile since someone's made
me feel this way.

Your hands never running a stray,
as you hold me tighter and tighter.

With every touch,
you take me higher.

As I sink into the melodies of your
choir.
My music grows inspired,
to the
igniting sensation of you.
Songwriter.

McKennah Noh

Thank you for surrounding me with your peace.
That you give to us with ease.

Your love's like a gentle breeze.
Soft and tender,
yet never failing to guide me.

Thank you for never giving up on me.
Thank you for helping me plant the seeds,
that will lead me to my fruit tree,
you have already claimed for me.

Ignition.
You ignite my soul with every transition,
slowly guiding my mind into submission.
No competition.

Your friction is my favorite prescription.
As you stop to listen,
to my rapid heart rendition.

You push me to different positions,
but you have my permission.
Your love's a limited edition.

Constantly pushing past the boundary conditions.
Indulging in our lover's diction.
You have me falling guilty of your love conviction.

McKennah Noh

Be picky with the seeds you let fall into your heart.
For that's where all of the growing starts.

Because there grows diverse and beautiful fine art.
Don't let anyone's weeds, tear your garden apart.

She's like a waterfall.
Wild, can't be tamed.

She erodes the toxic roots,
cleaning her surroundings away.

A force of her own,
tranquil from afar
but up close you'll see what she's always stood for.

Her currents are stronger
than one gives her credit for.
You'll feel her impact,
an impact you can't ignore.

McKennah Noh

The funny part is,
one day you'll be asked
to think of me and reminisce.
They'll look at me, then back at you
and ask you if you see it?

Confused you'll look at them and say "see what"?
Shaking their head slowly
they'll say clear cut…
"The chance you lost."

Diamonds.
They are a rare obsession.
They'll leave an everlasting impression.

So then why do people
lack to see the diamonds around them?
Overflowing in the everyday average person.

Diamonds are formed from oppression.
From people who didn't value their presence.
Diamonds are people of direction.
They are poised and know how to rise
from a recession.

So if you ever have the privilege of a diamond's essence.
You better sit down, listen,
and value them in the present.
Because when a diamond loves you count your blessing,
they'll fill you with a light as high as heaven.

I'm not a prize, put here to be won.
I'm not a toy. Put here for your fun.
Why play with my emotions inside?
In the end you won't see the begging
you say you don't desire but hide.

Unlike your perspective,
My goals shoot higher,
Past the typical societal desire.
I'm not the one to remorse who's left.
People do what they do,
I've gotten used to the tests.

They'll quiz you with promises,
seeing if you'll fall for them.
Seeing if you crumble the day,
they spit you out like chewing gum.

Become weightless words
that once held you to the ground,
kept you flying,
every time you hear their sound.

Within my walls, I protect a light,
that's meant for someone to forever hold tight.
Within these walls, I'll express my love,
to the one who shows me the answer
all of the above...

"*You're my gravitational pull*"
"*my equator*"
"*my equal sign*"

"*my want, not need*"
"*you're my heartbeat*"

— M

Like opposite magnets.
when they get too close,
they have no choice but to attract.

Love Embers

She was never hard to love, or hold, or listen to.

She just fulfilled the voids you never took the time to heal
before you pulled her into your broken worldview.

A view she tried to push you through,
but you pushed her away with not so little as a thank you.

So you didn't lose her
because she couldn't love or be there for you.

You lost her due to all the empty promises
and hurt you caused,
and can never undo.

McKennah Noh

Anywhere with you feels right.
I see home when I look into your eyes.

My bed doesn't feel the same if you're not by my side.
Your soul sets off an inner light.
It's so easy to stay up with you till midnight,
not even noticing how time passes by.

You have this way of teasing my smile lines,
the way they ache but it still satisfies
and I just picture the bliss of us dancing under the traffic lights.

Slowly illuminating our silhouettes
in shades of red, yellow, and green spotlights.
All of this is just the beginning to our highlights.

Just please never let me go,
Alright?

The art of kissing you...
In that first moment I knew,
the delicate way our lips
undue
the tension of our days waiting to break through.
Oh, how my lips never want to say adieu.

Every inch of you my body leans into.
As we wake with soft grace, to the morning dew,
watching your lips attend to,
every inch of my body
that waits for you.

Beautifully innocent our eyes say I love you...
As the late rosy air sways into
the windows of our bedroom.

Sharing the sweet remedies of earth's perfume.
As the morning fades to afternoon.
We lay in our blissful fortitude
looking for any excuse,
for our lips not to say
Adieu.

"*Say my name*" she said as she whispered sweet nothings.
Her weaknesses being magnified with every touch of his hands,
slowly gliding down the sweet silhouettes of her body.

As their souls danced together in the endless shades of midnight.
He paused and looked into her eyes…
both sinking deeper into each other's mindless electric currents.
Looking for each other's gentle reassurance,
that their passionate madness could last their endurance.

As the tension between their bodies begins to get heavy…
He responds with a voice so velvety,
"*Okay, baby.*"

Take a moment.
Be still.
Be as fluent as a breeze through a windmill.

Take a minute.
Look within.
Celebrate the hardships from which you've been.

Take a second.
Close your eyes.
Dream, envision, and fantasize.

Then go act and crystallize.

Most souls chase for happiness' embrace.
Later to find out
it could have always been there in the first place.

Like trying to glide on sand with skates,
you'll constantly feel misplaced.

So many forget to appreciate.
They hesitate to admit that it might be okay,
to be content in the dismay.

You see that's where the true warriors celebrate.
In the place of contentment, one finds the birthplace.
The birthplace of peace and grace.

Here souls never have to chase,
the temporary high of happiness's embrace.

Submerge in the evergreen with me...
where the air flows freely through the trees.

*Where we can grow old together
while our love never loses its leaves.*

Youthfully reflecting on the season's past.
Knowing that our souls are rooted in the Everlast.

McKennah Noh

The thing about love is that it's not just about you and me.
It's about the future of our family tree.

Think if we were to pause and think through the carefree,
of the true gratifying weight of love's responsibilities.

Yes, I want the cute little things,
but will you be there when the skies bring heavy rains?
That may twist harmony into hurricanes.

You see, love is more than the cute nicknames.
Love is the amount of work one puts into keeping it a flame.
Feeding each other's souls, not picking off remains.

This generation has turned love into a numbers game,
treating God's creation as if we were all the same.

What happened to the thrill of changing her maiden name?
Or taking the time to heal from what you've overcome.

Why do people continue to bond over toxic shame?
All that's doing is leaving cracks in the mainframe.

Smile.
You say religiously that you used to as a child.

Why has that changed to "every once in a while"
Your aura shines different when you smile.
Makes me feel warm to know
it's once again becoming a part of your lifestyle.

Speaking on your peace when you freestyle.
You've changed the narration of your profile.
Never missing a blessing single file.
I never get sick of your smile.

Within an entanglement I found my solution.
Our fingers danced between each other's
exchanging frequency distribution.

Getting lost in each other's illusions.

Feeling the heat of our fusion loosen,
into a beautiful stream of motion
that only you can find the resolution.

The way that our static builds up is traumatic.
Building in swells of waves so climatic,
yet flowing so real… so organic.

Your scent comforts me within the threads of your jacket.
Sick with your attraction, must be symptomatic.
Just entangled in a sporadic romantic.

I feel this lightness…
it embraces me with kind eyes.

It came at a fast pace, to my surprise,
given the weight of the past he helped me untie.
;
The strength of herself
gave her the courage to build what once was left on the ice shelf.
She took back from others what was always meant for herself.

This lightness doesn't come in swells.
She feels her cup constantly overflowing
forming consistent wells.

Oh, how the world can tell,
how happy she truly is
now.

Love Embers

My arms get jealous of the way your gloves can hold your
hands without having to let go.

My eyes ache at the fact that you can't see the way you glow,
always have me in awe trying to take mental photos.

My ears love the sound of your heart's tempo,
I turn you up every time I hear you on the radio.

Your soul seamlessly paints the blanks
of my canvas,
Michelangelo.

Your mind expands me like a rose of Jericho,
blooming to our manifesto.

— *Senses*

Fascinating how the same place
that was once a root of your pain,
can be the same place to close the chain
· that held one to the past.

Today, I found myself within those old halls,
this time though it was empty, but my heart wasn't.
It didn't hurt, which is good because I know I've grown,
but it still had bittersweet undertones.

To be in the same rooms that carried so much history,
but to the eye, one might just see empty desk seats,
not me…
I could still see where you said you loved me..
or even the times outside enjoying weather carefree.
Just young kids in "love", trying to get a degree.
We didn't know what the future would be.

I could still see the lessons that God had me unfolding.
Could still hear the monotonous voices
that would dance throughout the day.

But I could still see us.

I think it's worth discussing.
Sometimes people are told that it's detrimental
to revisit places or certain memories,
but wouldn't you if it's exactly what led you to your remedies?
Showing that you've grown into peace
with what once brought disparities.

Life will bring all sorts of seasons.
Each one will grow you, expand your vision.
Mine sure did…
So, as I walked in these old buildings that
housed that season,
I couldn't and wouldn't take back any of the
Teasing
Bleeding Feeling
or
Misleading greetings…

Because it led me to my freedom,
not in rights,
but in self-love
to be precise.

McKennah Noh

Some may say they've never felt love...
Or that they're too scared to, so why bother right?
Or they've fallen but into places
where a cold stillness caught their hearts
instead of the warmth...

I can say I've fallen to some of these outcomes,
and it's not pleasant,
but oh, does it make finding the true thing
so much more satiating.

I know I say this a lot,
that with you my effortless translation of my feelings
become shell shocked... speechless,
but with a calm peace I let it take me over.

Every inch of me wants to tell you though...
Wants to find the perfect words to match the incredible love that is
you...
So, this is me, trying to attempt just that.

"You took my heart... and gave it a home"
danced in our ears, filling our emotions with
an ecstasy of endless bliss.
It's something about your touch.
You're the first person that I know doesn't just feel me when the space
between us gets smaller and smaller,
you see me...
you hear me...
you hear every delicate caress,
telling you I love you.

You leave my lips in eloquent silence...
leaving every nerve, atom, cell in my being
wanting you even more,
frantically wanting to pass through every sensation
of raw, sweet, radiance I feel for you.

Love Embers

Out through the ends of my fingertips…
Into the coils of your hair
into the soft, safe warmth that is your chest…

Around the trusting fine drawn creases of your eyes…
as my fingertips kiss your skin,
surrendering to your soulful melody.
But it's nothing more than a silent scream…
that I hope you hear because my soul
doesn't know how else to tell you.

My eyes become overwhelmed with the surge of surrealism
that I let go…
I let my walls fall into you,
heavy with grace.
But you catch me and ever drop before one can hit your skin.

"I'm here baby", *"It's okay… I'm here"*
My breathing gets heavy, shaking with disbelief
that for once my soul feels relaxed hearing these words…
they're tired yet relieved tears.
Tears that have been shed for loving "too hard,"
tears that were taken for granted
tears now of joy…

I hold you as if you had just come back from war,
clinging to your heart that I hold so so dear to mine.
You make me want to be so close our energies become one.
It's just one beautiful flicker of light shining in unison.

Constantly outpouring the subdued walls to one another,
appreciating the firsts.

I've never been so comfortable in my skin
around anyone not even the mirror,
but with you I don't feel anything less of whole and safe.

Some may think to be naked you just help someone take off the layers of
clothing till there's a warm, plush layer which then means
you have seen all of that person.
Naked is the mask which clothes provide.
Eyes on the outside of these flowing walls of fabric
don't see the person they see exterior…
A bareness of soul and depth.
You haven't even seen the beginning of who they are.

What's their childhood street they played on till the streetlights went
off?
What thoughts keep them up till 2 am?
What's the stories laced within their scars, that they've never shown a
soul?
You haven't seen them naked… they were just covered with materialis-
tic wrapping that you ripped off abruptly.
As if they were the toy you wanted on Christmas
that you forgot was there 10 seconds after opening the next one.

"I don't want to cry but you know me so well"

The lyric hits me and I come back to the present,
touched by the reality that you are the first to ever see me.

To ever…
see
me.

All of me,
the me that is the most raw and vulnerable,
the me with painted stretch marks that kiss my thighs.
the me that has been loved, taken advantage of,
thrown away, and forgiven.

The incredible thing is…
I don't feel naked…
I don't have the immediate self-conciseness
to rush to the safety of darkness
to put my layers of walls back on.
"I actually could stay like this for a while"

Because for the first time having layers or not,
didn't mean anything to me…
you let me see you in the most open crease of your tender energy.

As did I…

Being there felt like a lifetime of different loves in one soul.
Forever in a moment.

First time I ever truly let someone see me naked…
stripped of insecurities now regrown with confidence and self-love.

So, thank you..

You took my heart…

And gave it a home…

So even though all I can manage to say in the moment

is
I love you.

Just know I tried to
give you something to
help you understand you,
from my

point
of
view…
I love you.

Love Embers

Honestly amazed at how the lines of life's story writing flow
seamlessly to a full circle.
With every curve one can think one chapter is done and over with,
but then at the next bound, life tells you otherwise.

Makes you wonder cluelessly in a moment,
then runs up to you on a regular January afternoon,
tugging at your jacket so you don't miss
the moment life's been waiting to show you.

The moment where the pain is no longer present,
rather it's a sweet calm,
a soothing new light to a shadow
you thought you knew the outcome of.

The moment where you stand shellshocked in warm surrealism,
from the sounds of shared laughter and smiles
you thought would never happen again.

The moment, it all
comes
together,
from what years ago, felt so far
a p a r t .

It's an overwhelming feeling of gratitude
mixed with a dash of confusion,
but the type of confusion where you try not to question
the reality of which life has brought you to,
but the confusion where you're just so damn happy and relieved
that it gave you the chance to read
the hidden new chapter of a bond
you thought was done.
— *thankful*

McKennah Noh

It was the same, but different?
This time in a really, really good way.

Conversation flowed with healing tides.
Tides that filled in the cracks that time wouldn't let us know before.

We weren't meant to know then and it's as clear as the rising horizon,
on a calm California day.
Funny you thought this is where I had moved away.

All I know is our narrative got this second chance on a weekday,
not by accident but from the way we were guided day to day.

Not forgetting to pray,
always for the other's family even on the rainy days.

I know my worth now and so do you.
Thank you for the lessons and thank you
for understanding my point of view.

What once was unanswered, unvalidated, and misconstrued,
is now shone in beautiful forgiveness never to be relived through.

It was a bittersweet warmth to be able to see you…
hug the one person I never would have thought I'd even want to,
again…
but it felt the same,
but this time,
with a vision from a brighter window frame.

A part of me knew all the lacing of our story would come undone
in the end.
When it had began,
you were a blast of refreshing perspective,
such an inquisitive mind,
the lanes of your thoughts were always aligned.

The over thinker falling for the one who already outgrew that
chapter.
I told you not to make promises when there was no pressure,
because deep down I think my intuition knew you'd forget
months soon after.

Intuition was right.
She'd always sit me down, trying to tell me that I was justified for
feeling the need to say
goodbye.
What once was safe energy,
stopped and replaced
with feelings of discomfort and flags you would slowly raise.

All the little things that added up to a over flowing maze
of which I came to the center of, on a regular March Saturday
resulting in the fact, that you never deserved
me.

McKennah Noh

What once were eyes of ease,
fell to be eyes that left me feeling empty and displeased,
at the fact that my body felt uncomfortable now within

1

2

3

Seconds that it be.
Yet you'd always say *"look at me"*

As If you felt it too within yourself,
that you were losing my fire,
diminishing my heat.
Losing my dilation that you let so easily slip away.
Fading into the shade,
where your effort and self reflection went astray.

So don't ever question why.
I walked away.
It was unfortunate,
your eyes didn't feel the same.

EPILOGUE

So here we are, two years later and it's crazy to say. In the moment, your soul takes in so many emotions you think it might never go away, but then you look in the mirror at a different reflection and realize that it's faded away. The pain, the uncertainty, the broken pieces...

They all just somehow picked themselves up and moved on to the spots within you they were always meant to go. Its funny, us humans think we truly know. Truly know how to maneuver through all life's funny jokes
that it'll throw at us, but the reality is, we don't.

It's a blessing really, who would want to live the perfect life?
Who would want a perfect love?
I wouldn't.

You would miss out on all the mistakes that led you to a better atmosphere. One where the air was clear and crisp and filled your lungs with new beginnings and blister filled lessons. They hurt and irritated you at first, making each breath hurt more and more, but then began to make room for new skin to grow, helping each breath, each movement flow, with ease, with peace. Then the next minute you look down, the blister is healed now.

Even though things are better, there will always be confrontation, awkward dinner table conversations, and concerned peers or parents. It's what you do when these things come that make thinking about the better, even better. Makes these ripples in the water come together, in a symphony that only your story can compose, for others to maybe relate to or hold close.

So, I hope you gained something from this snippet of my chapter, I know I did. I hope those parts of you you're too scared to look at, heal and are confronted because you deserve that.

You deserve the uncomfortable growth, and painful uneasy destinations because they'll lead you to what you've always wanted, and I wouldn't be doing you justice if I didn't challenge you to do so.

WE ALL DESERVE TO GROW.
EVERY ROSE HAS ITS
THORNS,
BUT IT'S STILL
AND ALWAYS
WILL BE,
BEAUTIFUL.

-MKN

UNAPOLOGETIC.

WHATEVER YOU ACCEPT ABOUT YOURSELF CAN-
NOT BE USED AGAINST YOU. BE WILLING TO OWN
YOUR TRUTH, EVEN IF IT MAKES OTHERS UNCOM-
FORTABLE. THE GOOD AND THE UGLY ARE ALL
PART OF YOUR STORY. YOU NEVER KNOW WHO YOU
CAN INSPIRE BY BEING YOUR AUTHENTIC, UNAPOL-
OGETICALLY SELF.

- Ash Alves

BUT AS FOR YOU,
BE STRONG
AND DO NOT GIVE UP,

FOR YOUR WORK WILL
BE REWARDED.

2 CHRONICLES 15:7

listen to POV on all platforms:
Spotify, SoundCloud, Apple Music

MCKENNAH NOH

pg. 157